Shakespeare, Ben Jonson, Beaumont and Fletcher

S. T. Coleridge

TABLE OF CONTENTS

Shakespeare

Definition Of Poetry.

Greek Drama.

Progress Of The Drama.

The Drama Generally, And Public Taste.

Shakespeare, A Poet Generally.

Shakespeare's Judgment equal to his Genius.

Recapitulation, And Summary Of the Characteristics of Shakespeare's Dramas.

Outline Of An Introductory Lecture Upon Shakespeare.

Order Of Shakespeare's Plays.

Notes On The "Tempest."

"Love's Labour's Lost."

"Midsummer Night's Dream."

"Comedy Of Errors."

"As You Like It."

"Twelfth Night."

"All's Well That Ends Well."

"Merry Wives Of Windsor."

"Measure For Measure."

"Cymbeline."

"Titus Andronicus."

"Troilus And Cressida."

"Coriolanus."

"Julius Cæsar."

"Antony And Cleopatra."

"Timon Of Athens."

"Romeo And Juliet."

Shakespeare's English Historical Plays.

"King John."

"Richard II."

"Henry IV.—Part I."

"Henry IV.—Part II."

"Henry V."

"Henry VI.—Part I."

"Richard III."

"Lear."

"Hamlet."

"Macbeth."

"Winter's Tale."

"Othello."

Notes on Ben Jonson.

Whalley's Preface.

"Whalley's 'Life Of Jonson.'"

"Every Man Out Of His Humour."

"Poetaster."

"Fall Of Sejanus."

"Volpone."

"Apicæne."

"The Alchemist."

"Catiline's Conspiracy."

"Bartholomew Fair."

"The Devil Is An Ass."

"The Staple Of News."

"The New Inn."

Notes On Beaumont And Fletcher.

Harris's Commendatory Poem On Fletcher.

Life Of Fletcher In Stockdale's Edition, 1811.

"Maid's Tragedy."

"A King And No King."

"The Scornful Lady."

"The Custom Of The Country."

"The Elder Brother."

"The Spanish Curate."

"Wit Without Money."

"The Humorous Lieutenant."

"The Mad Lover."

"The Loyal Subject."

"Rule A Wife And Have A Wife."

"The Laws Of Candy."

"The Little French Lawyer."

"Valentinian."

"Rollo."

"The Wildgoose Chase."

"A Wife For A Month."

"The Pilgrim."

"The Queen Of Corinth."

"The Noble Gentleman."

"The Coronation."

"Wit At Several Weapons."

"The Fair Maid Of The Inn."

"The Two Noble Kinsmen."

"The Woman Hater."

Shakespeare, With introductory matter on Poetry, the Drama, and the Stage.

Definition Of Poetry.

Poetry is not the proper antithesis to prose, but to science. Poetry is opposed to science, and prose to metre. The proper and immediate object of science is the acquirement, or communication, of truth; the proper and immediate object of poetry is the communication of immediate pleasure. This definition is useful; but as it would include novels and other works of fiction, which yet we do not call poems, there must be some additional character by which poetry is not only divided from opposites, but likewise distinguished from disparate, though similar, modes of composition. Now how is this to be effected? In animated prose, the beauties of nature, and the passions and accidents of human nature, are often expressed in that natural language which the contemplation of them would suggest to a pure and benevolent mind; yet still neither we nor the writers call such a work a poem, though no work could deserve that name which did not include all this, together with something else. What is this? It is that pleasurable emotion, that peculiar state and degree of excitement, which arises in the poet himself in the act of composition;—and in order to understand this, we must combine a more than ordinary sympathy with the objects, emotions, or incidents contemplated by the poet, consequent on a more than common sensibility, with a more than ordinary activity of the mind in respect of the fancy and the imagination. Hence is produced a more vivid reflection of the truths of nature and of the human heart, united with a constant activity modifying and correcting these truths by that sort of pleasurable emotion, which the exertion of all our faculties gives in a certain degree; but which can only be felt in perfection under the full play of those powers of mind, which are spontaneous rather than voluntary, and in which the effort required bears no proportion to the activity enjoyed. This is the state which permits the production of a highly pleasurable whole, of which each part shall also communicate for itself a distinct and conscious pleasure; and hence arises the definition, which I trust is now intelligible, that poetry, or rather a poem, is a species of composition, opposed to science, as having intellectual pleasure for its object, and as attaining its end by the use of language natural to us in a state of excitement,—but distinguished from other species of composition, not excluded by the former criterion, by permitting a pleasure from the whole consistent with a consciousness of pleasure from the component parts;—and the perfection of which is, to communicate from each part the greatest immediate pleasure compatible with the largest sum of pleasure on the whole. This, of course, will vary with the different modes of poetry;—and that splendour of particular lines, which would be worthy of admiration in an impassioned elegy, or a short indignant satire, would be a blemish and proof of vile taste in a tragedy or an epic poem.

It is remarkable, by the way, that Milton in three incidental words has implied all which for the purposes of more distinct apprehension, which at first must be slow-paced in order to be distinct, I have endeavoured to develope in a precise and strictly adequate definition. Speaking of poetry, he says, as in a parenthesis, "which is simple, sensuous, passionate." How awful is the power of words!—fearful often in their consequences when merely felt, not understood; but most awful when both felt and understood!—Had these three words only been properly understood by, and present in the minds of, general readers, not only almost a library of false poetry would have been either precluded or still-born, but, what is of more consequence, works truly excellent and capable of enlarging the understanding, warming and purifying the heart, and placing in the centre of the whole being the germs of noble and manlike actions, would have been the common diet of the intellect instead. For the first condition, simplicity,—while, on the one hand, it distinguishes poetry from the arduous processes of science, labouring towards an end not yet arrived at, and supposes a smooth and finished road, on which the reader is to walk onward easily, with streams murmuring by his side, and trees and flowers and human dwellings to make his journey as delightful as the object of it is desirable, instead of having to toil with the pioneers and painfully make the road on which others are to travel,—precludes, on the other hand, every affectation and morbid peculiarity;—the second condition, sensuousness, insures that framework of objectivity, that definiteness and articulation of imagery, and that modification of the images themselves, without which poetry becomes flattened into mere didactics of practice, or evaporated into a hazy, unthoughtful, day-dreaming; and the third condition, passion, provides that neither thought nor imagery shall be simply objective, but that the passio vera of humanity shall warm and animate both.

To return, however, to the previous definition, this most general and distinctive character of a poem originates in the poetic genius itself; and though it comprises whatever can with any propriety be called a poem (unless that word be a mere lazy synonym for a composition in metre), it yet becomes a just, and not merely discriminative, but full and adequate, definition of poetry in its highest and most peculiar sense, only so far as the distinction still results from the poetic genius, which sustains and modifies the emotions, thoughts, and vivid representations of the poem by the energy without effort of the poet's own mind,—by the spontaneous activity of his imagination and fancy, and by whatever else with these reveals itself in the balancing and reconciling of opposite or discordant qualities, sameness with difference, a sense of novelty and freshness with old or customary objects, a more than usual state of emotion with more than usual order, self-possession and judgment with enthusiasm and vehement feeling,—and which, while it blends and harmonizes the natural and the artificial, still subordinates art to nature, the manner to the matter, and our admiration of the poet to our sympathy with the images, passions, characters, and incidents of the poem:—

"Doubtless, this could not be, but that she turns
Bodies to spirit by sublimation strange,
As fire converts to fire the things it burns—
As we our food into our nature change!
"From their gross matter she abstracts their forms,
And draws a kind of quintessence from things,
Which to her proper nature she transforms
To bear them light on her celestial wings!
"Thus doth she, when from individual states
She doth abstract the universal kinds,
Which then reclothed in divers names and fates
Steal access thro' our senses to our minds."
Greek Drama.

It is truly singular that Plato,—whose philosophy and religion were but exotic at home, and a mere opposition to the finite in all things, genuine prophet and anticipator as he was of the Protestant Christian æra,—should have given in his Dialogue of the Banquet, a justification of our Shakespeare. For he relates that, when all the other guests had either dispersed or fallen asleep, Socrates only, together with Aristophanes and Agathon, remained awake, and that, while he continued to drink with them out of a large goblet, he compelled them, though most reluctantly, to admit that it was the business of one and the same genius to excel in tragic and comic poetry, or that the tragic poet ought, at the same time, to contain within himself the powers of comedy. Now, as this was directly repugnant to the entire theory of the ancient critics, and contrary to all their experience, it is evident that Plato must have fixed the eye of his contemplation on the innermost essentials of the drama, abstracted from the forms of age or country. In another passage he even adds the reason, namely, that opposites illustrate each other's nature, and in their struggle draw forth the strength of the combatants, and display the conqueror as sovereign even on the territories of the rival power.

Nothing can more forcibly exemplify the separative spirit of the Greek arts than their comedy as opposed to their tragedy. But as the immediate struggle of contraries supposes an arena common to both, so both were alike ideal; that is, the comedy of Aristophanes rose to as great a distance above the ludicrous of real life, as the tragedy of Sophocles above its tragic events and passions,—and it is in this one point, of absolute ideality, that the comedy of Shakespeare and the old comedy of Athens coincide. In this also alone did the Greek tragedy and comedy unite; in every thing else they were exactly opposed to each other. Tragedy is poetry in its deepest earnest; comedy is poetry in unlimited jest. Earnestness consists in the direction and convergence of all the powers of the soul to one aim, and in the voluntary restraint of its activity in consequence; the opposite, therefore, lies in the apparent abandonment of all definite aim or end, and in the removal of all bounds in the exercise of the mind,—attaining its real end, as an entire contrast, most perfectly, the greater the display is of intellectual wealth squandered in the wantonness of sport without an object, and the more abundant the life and vivacity in the creations of the arbitrary will.

The later comedy, even where it was really comic, was doubtless likewise more comic, the more free it appeared from any fixed aim. Misunderstandings of intention, fruitless struggles of absurd passion, contradictions of temper, and laughable situations there were; but still the form of the representation itself was serious; it proceeded as much according to settled laws, and used as much the same means of art, though to a different purpose, as the regular tragedy itself. But in the old comedy the very form itself is whimsical; the whole work is one great jest, comprehending a world of jests within it, among which each maintains its own place without seeming to concern itself as to the relation in which it may stand to its fellows. In short, in Sophocles, the constitution of tragedy is monarchical, but such as it existed in elder Greece, limited by laws, and therefore the more venerable,—all the parts adapting and submitting themselves to the majesty of the heroic sceptre:—in Aristophanes, comedy, on the contrary, is poetry in its most democratic form, and it is a fundamental principle with it, rather to risk all the confusion of anarchy, than to destroy the independence and privileges of its individual constituents,—place, verse, characters, even single thoughts, conceits, and allusions, each turning on the pivot of its own free will.

The tragic poet idealizes his characters by giving to the spiritual part of our nature a more decided preponderance over the animal cravings and impulses, than is met with in real life: the comic poet idealizes his characters by making the animal the governing power, and the intellectual the mere instrument. But as tragedy is not a collection of virtues and perfections, but takes care only that the vices and imperfections shall spring from the passions, errors, and prejudices which arise out of the soul;—so neither is comedy a mere crowd of vices and follies, but whatever qualities it represents, even though they are in a certain sense amiable, it still displays them as having their origin in some dependence on our lower nature, accompanied with a defect in true freedom of spirit and self-subsistence, and subject to that unconnection by contradictions of the inward being, to which all folly is owing.

The ideal of earnest poetry consists in the union and harmonious melting down, and fusion of the sensual into the spiritual,—of man as an animal into man as a power of reason and self-government. And this we have represented to us most clearly in the plastic art, or statuary; where the perfection of outward form is a symbol of the perfection of an inward idea; where the body is wholly penetrated by the soul, and spiritualized even to a state of glory, and like a transparent substance, the matter, in its own nature darkness, becomes altogether a vehicle and fixture of light, a means of developing its beauties, and unfolding its wealth of various colours without disturbing its unity, or causing a division of the parts. The sportive ideal, on the contrary, consists in the perfect harmony and concord of the higher nature with the animal, as with its ruling principle and its acknowledged regent. The understanding and practical reason are represented as the willing slaves of the senses and appetites, and of the passions arising out of them. Hence we may admit the appropriateness to the old comedy, as a work of defined art, of allusions and descriptions, which morality can never justify, and, only with reference to the author himself, and only as being the effect or rather the cause of the circumstances in which he wrote, can consent even to palliate.

The old comedy rose to its perfection in Aristophanes, and in him also it died with the freedom of Greece. Then arose a species of drama, more fitly called dramatic entertainment than comedy, but of which, nevertheless, our modern comedy (Shakespeare's altogether excepted) is the genuine descendant. Euripides had already brought tragedy lower down and by many steps nearer to the real world than his predecessors had ever done, and the passionate admiration which Menander and Philemon expressed for him, and their open avowals that he was their great master, entitle us to consider their dramas as of a middle species, between tragedy and comedy,—not the tragi-comedy, or thing of heterogeneous parts, but a complete whole, founded on principles of its own. Throughout we find the drama of Menander distinguishing itself from tragedy, but not as the genuine old comedy, contrasting with, and opposing it. Tragedy, indeed, carried the thoughts into the mythologic world, in order to raise the emotions, the fears, and the hopes, which convince the inmost heart that their final cause is not to be discovered in the limits of mere mortal life, and force us into a presentiment, however dim, of a state in which those struggles of inward free will with outward necessity, which form the true subject of the tragedian, shall be reconciled and solved;—the entertainment or new comedy, on the other hand, remained within the circle of experience. Instead of the tragic destiny, it introduced the power of chance; even in the few fragments of Menander and Philemon now remaining to us, we find many exclamations and reflections concerning chance and fortune, as in the tragic poets concerning destiny. In tragedy, the moral law, either as obeyed or violated, above all consequences—its own maintenance or violation constituting the most important of all consequences—forms the ground; the new comedy, and our modern comedy in general (Shakespeare excepted as before) lies in prudence or imprudence, enlightened or misled self-love. The whole moral system of the entertainment exactly like that of fable, consists in rules of prudence, with an exquisite conciseness, and at the same time an exhaustive fulness of sense. An old critic said that tragedy was the flight or elevation of life, comedy (that of Menander) its arrangement or ordonnance.

Add to these features a portrait-like truth of character,—not so far indeed as that a bona fide individual should be described or imagined, but yet so that the features which give interest and permanence to the class should be individualized. The old tragedy moved in an ideal world,—the old comedy in a fantastic world. As the entertainment, or new comedy, restrained the creative activity both of the fancy and the imagination, it indemnified the understanding in appealing to the judgment for the probability of the scenes represented. The ancients themselves acknowledged the new comedy as an exact copy of real life. The grammarian, Aristophanes, somewhat affectedly exclaimed:—"O Life and Menander! which of you two imitated the other?" In short the form of this species of drama was poetry, the stuff or matter was prose. It was prose rendered delightful by the blandishments and measured motions of the muse. Yet even this was not universal. The mimes of Sophron, so passionately admired by Plato, were written in prose, and were scenes out of real life conducted in dialogue. The exquisite feast of Adonis (Συρακούσιαι ἢ Ἀδωνιάζουσαι) in Theocritus, we are told, with some others of his eclogues, were close imitations of certain mimes of Sophron—free translations of the prose into hexameters.

It will not be improper, in this place, to make a few remarks on the remarkable character and functions of the chorus in the Greek tragic drama.

The chorus entered from below, close by the orchestra, and there, pacing to and fro during the choral odes, performed their solemn measured dance. In the centre of the orchestra, directly over against the middle of the scene, there stood an elevation with steps in the shape of a large altar, as high as the boards of the logeion or moveable stage. This elevation was named the thymele (θυμέλη), and served to recall the origin and original purpose of the chorus, as an altar-song in honour of the presiding deity. Here, and on these steps the persons of the chorus sate collectively, when they were not singing; attending to the dialogue as spectators, and acting as (what in truth they were) the ideal representatives of the real audience, and of the poet himself in his own character, assuming the supposed impressions made by the drama, in order to direct and rule them. But when the chorus itself formed part of the dialogue, then the leader of the band, the foreman, or coryphæus, ascended, as some think, the level summit of the thymele in order to command the stage, or, perhaps, the whole chorus advanced to the front of the orchestra, and thus put themselves in ideal connection, as it were, with the dramatis personæ there acting. This thymele was in the centre of the whole edifice, all the measurements were calculated, and the semi-circle of the amphitheatre was drawn from this point. It had a double use, a twofold purpose; it constantly reminded the spectators of the origin of tragedy as a religious service, and declared itself as the ideal representative of the audience by having its place exactly in the point, to which all the radii from the different seats or benches converged.

In this double character, as constituent parts, and yet at the same time as spectators, of the drama, the chorus could not but tend to enforce the unity of place;—not on the score of any supposed improbability, which the understanding or common sense might detect in a change of place;—but because the senses themselves put it out of the power of any imagination to conceive a place coming to, and going away from the persons, instead of the persons changing their place. Yet there are instances, in which, during the silence of the chorus, the poets have hazarded this by a change in that part of the scenery which represented the more distant objects to the eye of the spectator—a demonstrative proof, that this alternately extolled and ridiculed unity (as ignorantly ridiculed as extolled) was grounded on no essential principle of reason, but arose out of circumstances which the poet could not remove, and therefore took up into the form of the drama, and co-organised it with all the other parts into a living whole.

The Greek tragedy may rather be compared to our serious opera than to the tragedies of Shakespeare; nevertheless, the difference is far greater than the likeness. In the opera all is subordinated to the music, the dresses, and the scenery;—the poetry is a mere vehicle for articulation, and as little pleasure is lost by ignorance of the Italian language, so is little gained by the knowledge of it. But in the Greek drama all was but as instruments and accessaries to the poetry; and hence we should form a better notion of the choral music from the solemn hymns and psalms of austere church music than from any species of theatrical singing. A single flute or pipe was the ordinary accompaniment; and it is not to be supposed, that any display of musical power was allowed to obscure the distinct hearing of the words. On the contrary, the evident purpose was to render the words more audible, and to secure by the elevations and pauses greater facility of understanding the poetry. For the choral songs are, and ever must have been, the most difficult part of the tragedy; there occur in them the most involved verbal compounds, the newest expressions, the boldest images, the most recondite allusions. Is it credible that the poets would, one and all, have been thus prodigal of the stores of art and genius, if they had known that in the representation the whole must have been lost to the audience,—at a time too, when the means of after publication were so difficult and expensive, and the copies of their works so slowly and narrowly circulated?

The masks also must be considered—their vast variety and admirable workmanship. Of this we retain proof by the marble masks which represented them; but to this in the real mask we must add the thinness of the substance and the exquisite fitting on to the head of the actor; so that not only were the very eyes painted with a single opening left for the pupil of the actor's eye, but in some instances, even the iris itself was painted, when the colour was a known characteristic of the divine or heroic personage represented.

Finally, I will note down those fundamental characteristics which contradistinguish the ancient literature from the modern generally, but which more especially appear in prominence in the tragic drama. The ancient was allied to statuary, the modern refers to painting. In the first there is a predominance of rhythm and melody, in the second of harmony and counterpoint. The Greeks idolized the finite, and therefore were the masters of all grace, elegance, proportion, fancy, dignity, majesty—of whatever, in short, is capable of being definitely conveyed by defined forms or thoughts: the moderns revere the infinite, and affect the indefinite as a vehicle of the infinite;—hence their passions, their obscure hopes and fears, their wandering through the unknown, their grander moral feelings, their more august conception of man as man, their future rather than their past—in a word, their sublimity.

Progress Of The Drama.

Let two persons join in the same scheme to ridicule a third, and either take advantage of, or invent, some story for that purpose, and mimicry will have already produced a sort of rude comedy. It becomes an inviting treat to the populace, and gains an additional zest and burlesque by following the already established plan of tragedy; and the first man of genius who seizes the idea, and reduces it into form,—into a work of art,—by metre and music, is the Aristophanes of the country.

How just this account is will appear from the fact that in the first or old comedy of the Athenians, most of the dramatis personæ were living characters introduced under their own names; and no doubt, their ordinary dress, manner, person and voice were closely mimicked. In less favourable states of society, as that of England in the middle ages, the beginnings of comedy would be constantly taking place from the mimics and satirical minstrels; but from want of fixed abode, popular government, and the successive attendance of the same auditors, it would still remain in embryo. I shall, perhaps, have occasion to observe that this remark is not without importance in explaining the essential differences of the modern and ancient theatres.

Phenomena, similar to those which accompanied the origin of tragedy and comedy among the Greeks, would take place among the Romans much more slowly, and the drama would, in any case, have much longer remained in its first irregular form from the character of the people, their continual engagements in wars of conquest, the nature of their government, and their rapidly increasing empire. But, however this might have been, the conquest of

Greece precluded both the process and the necessity of it; and the Roman stage at once presented imitations or translations of the Greek drama. This continued till the perfect establishment of Christianity. Some attempts, indeed, were made to adapt the persons of Scriptural or ecclesiastical history to the drama; and sacred plays, it is probable, were not unknown in Constantinople under the emperors of the East. The first of the kind is, I believe, the only one preserved,—namely, the Χριστὸς Πάσχων, or, "Christ in his sufferings," by Gregory Nazianzen,—possibly written in consequence of the prohibition of profane literature to the Christians by the apostate Julian. In the West, however, the enslaved and debauched Roman world became too barbarous for any theatrical exhibitions more refined than those of pageants and chariot-races; while the spirit of Christianity, which in its most corrupt form still breathed general humanity, whenever controversies of faith were not concerned, had done away the cruel combats of the gladiators, and the loss of the distant provinces prevented the possibility of exhibiting the engagements of wild beasts.

I pass, therefore, at once to the feudal ages which soon succeeded, confining my observation to this country; though, indeed, the same remark with very few alterations will apply to all the other states, into which the great empire was broken. Ages of darkness succeeded;—not, indeed, the darkness of Russia or of the barbarous lands unconquered by Rome; for from the time of Honorius to the destruction of Constantinople and the consequent introduction of ancient literature into Europe, there was a continued succession of individual intellects;—the golden chain was never wholly broken, though the connecting links were often of baser metal. A dark cloud, like another sky, covered the entire cope of heaven,—but in this place it thinned away, and white stains of light showed a half eclipsed star behind it,—in that place it was rent asunder, and a star passed across the opening in all its brightness, and then vanished. Such stars exhibited themselves only; surrounding objects did not partake of their light. There were deep wells of knowledge, but no fertilizing rills and rivulets. For the drama, society was altogether a state of chaos, out of which it was, for a while at least, to proceed anew, as if there had been none before it. And yet it is not undelightful to contemplate the education of good from evil. The ignorance of the great mass of our countrymen was the efficient cause of the reproduction of the drama; and the preceding darkness and the returning light were alike necessary in order to the creation of a Shakespeare.

The drama re-commenced in England, as it first began in Greece, in religion. The people were not able to read,—the priesthood were unwilling that they should read; and yet their own interest compelled them not to leave the people wholly ignorant of the great events of sacred history. They did that, therefore, by scenic representations, which in after ages it has been attempted to do in Roman Catholic countries by pictures. They presented Mysteries, and often at great expense; and reliques of this system still remain in the south of Europe, and indeed throughout Italy, where at Christmas the convents and the great nobles rival each other in the scenic representation of the birth of Christ and its circumstances. I heard two instances mentioned to me at different times, one in Sicily and the other in Rome, of noble devotees, the ruin of whose fortunes was said to have commenced in the extravagant expense which had been incurred in presenting the præsepe or manger. But these Mysteries, in order to answer their design, must not only be instructive, but entertaining; and as, when they became so, the people began to take pleasure in acting them themselves—in interloping—(against which the priests seem to have fought hard and yet in vain) the most ludicrous images were mixed with the most awful personations; and whatever the subject might be, however sublime, however pathetic, yet the Vice and the Devil, who are the genuine antecessors of Harlequin and the Clown, were necessary component parts. I have myself a piece of this kind, which I transcribed a few years ago at Helmstadt, in Germany, on the education of Eve's children, in which after the fall and repentance of Adam, the offended Maker, as in proof of his reconciliation, condescends to visit them, and to catechise the children,—who with a noble contempt of chronology are all brought together from Abel to Noah. The good children say the ten Commandments, the Belief, and the Lord's Prayer; but Cain and his rout, after he had received a box on the ear for not taking off his hat, and afterwards offering his left hand, is prompted by the devil so to blunder in the Lord's Prayer as to reverse the petitions and say it backward!

Unaffectedly I declare I feel pain at repetitions like these, however innocent. As historical documents they are valuable; but I am sensible that what I can read with my eye with perfect innocence, I cannot without inward fear and misgivings pronounce with my tongue.

Let me, however, be acquitted of presumption if I say that I cannot agree with Mr. Malone, that our ancestors did not perceive the ludicrous in these things, or that they paid no separate attention to the serious and comic parts. Indeed his own statement contradicts it. For what purpose should the Vice leap upon the Devil's back and belabour him, but to produce this separate attention? The people laughed heartily, no doubt. Nor can I conceive any meaning attached to the words "separate attention," that is not fully answered by one part of an exhibition exciting seriousness or pity, and the other raising mirth and loud laughter. That they felt no impiety in the affair is most true. For it is the very essence of that system of Christian polytheism, which in all its essentials is now fully as gross in Spain, in Sicily, and the South of Italy, as it ever was in England in the days of Henry VI. (nay, more so, for a Wicliffe had not then appeared only, but scattered the good seed widely),—it is an essential part, I say, of that system to draw the mind wholly from its own inward whispers and quiet discriminations, and to habituate the conscience to pronounce sentence in every case according to the established verdicts of the church and the casuists. I have looked through volume after volume of the most approved casuists,—and still I find disquisitions whether this or that act is right, and under what circumstances, to a minuteness that makes reasoning ridiculous, and of a callous and unnatural immodesty, to which none but a monk could harden himself, who has been stripped of all the tender charities of life, yet is goaded on to make war against them by the unsubdued hauntings of our meaner nature, even as dogs are said to get the hydrophobia from excessive thirst. I fully believe that our ancestors laughed as heartily, as their posterity do at Grimaldi;—and not having been told that they would be punished for laughing, they thought it very innocent;—and if their priests had left out murder in the catalogue of their prohibitions (as indeed they did under certain circumstances of heresy), the greater part of them,—the moral instincts common to all men having been smothered and kept from development,—would have thought as little of murder.

However this may be, the necessity of at once instructing and gratifying the people produced the great distinction between the Greek and the English theatres;—for to this we must attribute the origin of tragi-comedy, or a representation of human events more lively, nearer the truth, and permitting a larger field of moral instruction, a more ample exhibition of the recesses of the human heart, under all the trials and circumstances that most concern us, than was known or guessed at by Æschylus, Sophocles, or Euripides;—and at the same time we learn to account for, and—relatively to the author—perceive the necessity of, the Fool or Clown or both, as the substitutes of the Vice and the Devil, which our ancestors had been so accustomed to see in every exhibition of the stage, that they could not feel any performance perfect without them. Even to this day in Italy, every opera—(even Metastasio obeyed the claim throughout)—must have six characters, generally two pairs of cross lovers, a tyrant and a confidant, or a father and two confidants, themselves lovers;—and when a new opera appears, it is the universal fashion to ask—which is the tyrant, which the lover? &c.

It is the especial honour of Christianity, that in its worst and most corrupted form it cannot wholly separate itself from morality;—whereas the other religions in their best form (I do not include Mohammedanism, which is only an anomalous corruption of Christianity, like Swedenborgianism) have no connection with it. The very impersonation of moral evil under the name of Vice, facilitated all other impersonations; and hence we see that the Mysteries were succeeded by Moralities, or dialogues and plots of allegorical personages. Again, some character in real history had become so famous, so proverbial, as Nero for instance, that they were introduced instead of the moral quality, for which they were so noted;—and in this manner the stage was moving on to the absolute production of heroic and comic real characters, when the restoration of literature, followed by the ever-blessed Reformation, let in upon the kingdom not only new knowledge, but new motive. A useful rivalry commenced between the metropolis on the one hand,—the residence, independently of the court and nobles, of the most active and stirring spirits who had not been regularly educated, or who, from mischance or otherwise, had forsaken the beaten track of preferment,—and the universities on the other. The latter prided themselves on their closer approximation to the ancient rules and ancient regularity—taking the theatre of Greece, or rather its dim reflection, the rhetorical tragedies of the poet Seneca, as a perfect ideal, without any critical collation of the times, origin, or circumstances;—whilst, in the mean time, the popular writers, who could not and would not abandon what they had found to delight their countrymen sincerely, and not merely from inquiries first put to the recollection of rules, and answered in the affirmative, as if it had been an arithmetical sum, did yet borrow from the scholars whatever they advantageously could, consistently with their own peculiar means of pleasing.

And here let me pause for a moment's contemplation of this interesting subject.

We call, for we see and feel, the swan and the dove both transcendantly beautiful. As absurd as it would be to institute a comparison between their separate claims to beauty from any abstract rule common to both, without reference to the life and being of the animals themselves,—or as if, having first seen the dove, we abstracted its outlines, gave them a false generalization, called them the principles or ideal of bird-beauty, and then proceeded to criticise the swan or the eagle;—not less absurd is it to pass judgment on the works of a poet on the mere ground that they have been called by the same class-name with the works of other poets in other times and circumstances, or on any ground, indeed, save that of their inappropriateness to their own end and being, their want of significance, as symbols or physiognomy.

O! few have there been among critics, who have followed with the eye of the imagination the imperishable yet ever wandering spirit of poetry through its various metempsychoses, and consequent metamorphoses;—or who have rejoiced in the light of clear perception at beholding with each new birth, with each rare avatar, the human race frame to itself a new body, by assimilating materials of nourishment out of its new circumstances, and work for itself new organs of power appropriate to the new sphere of its motion and activity!

I have before spoken of the Romance, or the language formed out of the decayed Roman and the Northern tongues; and comparing it with the Latin, we find it less perfect in simplicity and relation—the privileges of a language formed by the mere attraction of homogeneous parts;—but yet more rich, more expressive and various, as one formed by more obscure affinities out of a chaos of apparently heterogeneous atoms. As more than a metaphor,—as an analogy of this, I have named the true genuine modern poetry the romantic; and the works of Shakespeare are romantic poetry, revealing itself in the drama. If the tragedies of Sophocles are in the strict sense of the word tragedies, and the comedies of Aristophanes comedies, we must emancipate ourselves from a false association arising from misapplied names, and find a new word for the plays of Shakespeare. For they are, in the ancient sense, neither tragedies nor comedies, nor both in one,—but a different genus, diverse in kind, and not merely different in degree. They may be called romantic dramas, or dramatic romances.

A deviation from the simple forms and unities of the ancient stage is an essential principle, and, of course, an appropriate excellence, of the romantic drama. For these unities were to a great extent the natural form of that which in its elements was homogeneous, and the representation of which was addressed pre-eminently to the outward senses;—and though the fable, the language, and the characters appealed to the reason rather than to the mere understanding, inasmuch as they supposed an ideal state rather than referred to an existing reality,—yet it was a reason which was obliged to accommodate itself to the senses, and so far became a sort of more elevated understanding. On the other hand, the romantic poetry—the Shakespearian drama—appealed to the imagination rather than to the senses, and to the reason as contemplating our inward nature, and the workings of the passions in their most retired recesses. But the reason, as reason, is independent of time and space; it has nothing to do with them: and hence the certainties of reason have been called eternal truths. As for example—the endless properties of the circle:—what connection have they with this or that age, with this or that country?—The reason is aloof from time and space; the imagination is an arbitrary controller over both;—and if only the poet have such power of exciting our internal emotions as to make us present to the scene in imagination chiefly, he acquires the right and privilege of using time and space as they exist in imagination, and obedient only to the laws by which the imagination itself acts. These laws it will be my object and aim to point out as the examples occur, which illustrate them. But here let me remark what can never be too often reflected on by all who would intelligently study the works either of the Athenian dramatists, or of Shakespeare, that the very essence of the former consists in the sternest separation of the diverse in kind and the disparate in the degree, whilst the latter delights in interlacing, by a rainbow-like transfusion of hues, the one with the other.

And here it will be necessary to say a few words on the stage and on stage-illusion.

A theatre, in the widest sense of the word, is the general term for all places of amusement through the ear or eye, in which men assemble in order to be amused by some entertainment presented to all at the same time and in common. Thus an old Puritan divine says:—"Those who attend public worship and sermons only to amuse themselves, make a theatre of the church, and turn God's house into the devil's. Theatra ædes diabololatricæ." The most important and dignified species of this genus is, doubtless, the stage (res theatralis histrionica), which, in addition to the generic definition above given, may be characterized in its idea, or according to what it does, or ought to, aim at, as a combination of several or of all the fine arts in an harmonious whole, having a distinct end of its own, to which the peculiar end of each of the component arts, taken separately, is made subordinate and subservient,—that, namely, of imitating reality—whether external things, actions, or passions—under a semblance of reality. Thus, Claude imitates a landscape at sunset, but only as a picture; while a forest-scene is not presented to the spectators as a picture, but as a forest; and though, in the full sense of the word, we are no more deceived by the one than by the other, yet are our feelings very differently affected; and the pleasure derived from the one is not composed of the same elements as that afforded by the other, even on the supposition that the quantum of both were equal. In the former, a picture, it is a condition of all genuine delight that we should not be deceived; in the latter, stage-scenery (inasmuch as its principle end is not in or for itself, as is the case in a picture, but to be an assistance and means to an end out of itself), its very purpose is to produce as much illusion as its nature permits. These, and all other stage presentations, are to produce a sort of temporary half-faith, which the spectator encourages in himself and supports by a voluntary contribution on his own part, because he knows that it is at all times in his power to see the thing as it really is. I have often observed that little children are actually deceived by stage-scenery, never by pictures; though even these produce an effect on their impressible minds, which they do not on the minds of adults. The child, if strongly impressed, does not indeed positively think the picture to be the reality; but yet he does not think the contrary. As Sir George Beaumont was shewing me a very fine engraving from Rubens, representing a storm at sea without any vessel or boat introduced, my little boy, then about five years old, came dancing and singing into the room, and all at once (if I may so say) tumbled in upon the print. He instantly started, stood silent and motionless, with the strongest expression, first of wonder and then of grief in his eyes and countenance, and at length said "And where is the ship? But that is sunk, and the men are all drowned!" still keeping his eyes fixed on the print. Now what pictures are to little children, stage illusion is to men, provided they retain any part of the child's sensibility; except, that in the latter instance, the suspension of the act of comparison, which permits this sort of negative belief, is somewhat more assisted by the will, than in that of a child respecting a picture.

The true stage-illusion in this and in all other things consists—not in the mind's judging it to be a forest, but, in its remission of the judgment that it is not a forest. And this subject of stage-illusion is so important, and so many practical errors and false criticisms may arise, and indeed have arisen, either from reasoning on it as actual delusion (the strange notion, on which the French critics built up their theory, and on which the French poets justify the construction of their tragedies), or from denying it altogether (which seems the end of Dr. Johnson's reasoning, and which, as extremes meet, would lead to the very same consequences, by excluding whatever would not be judged probable by us in our coolest state of feeling, with all our faculties in even balance), that these few remarks will, I hope, be pardoned, if they should serve either to explain or to illustrate the point. For not only are we never absolutely deluded—or any thing like it, but the attempt to cause the highest delusion possible to beings in their senses sitting in a theatre, is a gross fault, incident only to low minds, which, feeling that they cannot affect the heart or head permanently, endeavour to call forth the momentary affections. There ought never to be more pain than is compatible with coexisting pleasure, and to be amply repaid by thought.

Shakespeare found the infant stage demanding an intermixture of ludicrous character as imperiously as that of Greece did the chorus, and high language accordant. And there are many advantages in this;—a greater assimilation to nature, a greater scope of power, more truths, and more feelings;—the effects of contrast, as in Lear and the Fool; and especially this, that the true language of passion becomes sufficiently elevated by your having previously heard, in the same piece, the lighter conversation of men under no strong emotion. The very nakedness of the stage, too, was advantageous,—for the drama thence became something between recitation and a representation; and the absence or paucity of scenes allowed a freedom from the laws of unity of place and unity of time, the observance of which must either confine the drama to as few subjects as may be counted on the fingers, or involve gross improbabilities, far more striking than the violation would have caused. Thence, also, was precluded the danger of a false ideal,—of aiming at more than what is possible on the whole. What play of the ancients, with reference to their ideal, does not hold out more glaring absurdities than any in Shakespeare? On the Greek plan a man could more easily be a poet than a dramatist; upon our plan more easily a dramatist than a poet.

The Drama Generally, And Public Taste.

Unaccustomed to address such an audience, and having lost by a long interval of confinement the advantages of my former short schooling, I had miscalculated in my last Lecture the proportion of my matter to my time, and by bad economy and unskilful management, the several heads of my discourse failed in making the entire performance correspond with the promise publicly circulated in the weekly annunciation of the subjects to be treated. It would indeed have been wiser in me, and perhaps better on the whole, if I had caused my Lectures to be announced only as continuations of the main subject. But if I be, as perforce I must be, gratified by the recollection of whatever has appeared to give you pleasure, I am conscious of something better, though less flattering, a sense of unfeigned gratitude for your forbearance with my defects. Like affectionate guardians, you see without disgust the awkwardness, and witness with sympathy the growing pains, of a youthful endeavour, and look forward with a hope, which is its own reward, to the contingent results of practice—to its intellectual maturity.

In my last address I defined poetry to be the art, or whatever better term our language may afford, of representing external nature and human thoughts, both relatively to human affections, so as to cause the production of as great immediate pleasure in each part, as is compatible with the largest possible sum of pleasure on the whole. Now this definition applies equally to painting and music as to poetry; and in truth the term poetry is alike applicable to all three. The vehicle alone constitutes the difference; and the term "poetry" is rightly applied by eminence to measured words, only because the sphere of their action is far wider, the power of giving permanence to them much more certain, and incomparably greater the facility, by which men, not defective by nature or disease, may be enabled to derive habitual pleasure and instruction from them. On my mentioning these considerations to a painter of great genius, who had been, from a most honourable enthusiasm, extolling his own art, he was so struck with their truth, that he exclaimed, "I want no other arguments;—poetry, that is, verbal poetry, must be the greatest; all that proves final causes in the world, proves this; it would be shocking to think otherwise!"—And in truth, deeply, O! far more than words can express, as I venerate the Last Judgment and the Prophets of Michel Angelo Buonarotti,—yet the very pain which I repeatedly felt as I lost myself in gazing upon them, the painful consideration that their having been painted in fresco was the sole cause that they had not been abandoned to all the accidents of a dangerous transportation to a distant capital, and that the same caprice, which made the Neapolitan soldiery destroy all the exquisite masterpieces on the walls of the church of Trinitado Monte, after the retreat of their antagonist barbarians, might as easily have made vanish the rooms and open gallery of Raffael, and the yet more unapproachable wonders of the sublime Florentine in the Sixtine Chapel, forced upon my mind the reflection: How grateful the human race ought to be that the works of Euclid, Newton, Plato, Milton, Shakespeare, are not subjected to similar contingencies,—that they and their fellows, and the great, though inferior, peerage of undying intellect, are secured;—secured even from a second irruption of Goths and Vandals, in addition to many other safeguards, by the vast empire of English language, laws, and religion founded in America, through the overflow of the power and the virtue of my country;—and that now the great and certain works of genuine fame can only cease to act for mankind, when men themselves cease to be men, or when the planet on which they exist, shall have altered its relations, or have ceased to be. Lord Bacon, in the language of the gods, if I may use an Homeric phrase, has expressed a similar thought:—

"Lastly, leaving the vulgar arguments, that by learning man excelleth man in that wherein man excelleth beasts; that by learning man ascendeth to the heavens and their motions, where in body he cannot come, and the like; let us conclude with the dignity and excellency of knowledge and learning in that whereunto man's nature doth most aspire, which is immortality or continuance: for to this tendeth generation, and raising of houses and families; to this tend buildings, foundations, and monuments; to this tendeth the desire of memory, fame, and celebration, and in effect the strength of all other human desires. We see then how far the monuments of wit and learning are more durable than the monuments of power, or of the hands. For have not the verses of Homer continued twenty-five hundred years, or more, without the loss of a syllable or letter; during which time, infinite palaces, temples, castles, cities, have been decayed and demolished? It is not possible to have the true pictures or statues of Cyrus, Alexander, Cæsar; no, nor of the kings or great personages of much later years; for the originals cannot last, and the copies cannot but lose of the life and truth. But the images of men's wits and knowledges remain in books, exempted from the wrong of time, and capable of perpetual renovation. Neither are they fitly to be called images, because they generate still, and cast their seeds in the minds of others, provoking and causing infinite actions and opinions in succeeding ages: so that, if the invention of the ship was thought so noble, which carrieth riches and commodities from place to place, and consociateth the most remote regions in participation of their fruits; how much more are letters to be magnified, which, as ships, pass through the vast seas of time, and make ages so distant to participate of the wisdom, illuminations, and inventions, the one of the other?"

But let us now consider what the drama should be. And first, it is not a copy, but an imitation, of nature. This is the universal principle of the fine arts. In all well laid out grounds what delight do we feel from that balance and antithesis of feelings and thoughts! How natural! we say;—but the very wonder that caused the exclamation, implies that we perceived art at the same moment. We catch the hint from nature itself. Whenever in mountains or cataracts we discover a likeness to any thing artificial which yet we know is not artificial—what pleasure! And so it is in appearances known to be artificial, which appear to be natural. This applies in due degrees, regulated by steady good sense, from a clump of trees to the Paradise Lost or Othello. It would be easy to apply it to painting and even, though with greater abstraction of thought, and by more subtle yet equally just analogies—to music. But this belongs to others; suffice it that one great principle is common to all the fine arts, a principle which probably is the condition of all consciousness, without which we should feel and imagine only by discontinuous moments, and be plants or brute animals instead of men;—I mean that ever-varying balance, or balancing, of images, notions, or feelings, conceived as in opposition to each other;—in short, the perception of identity and contrariety; the least degree of which constitutes likeness, the greatest absolute difference; but the infinite gradations between these two form all the play and all the interest of our intellectual and moral being, till it leads us to a feeling and an object more awful than it seems to me compatible with even the present subject to utter aloud, though I am most desirous to suggest it. For there alone are all things at once different and the same; there alone, as the principle of all things, does distinction exist unaided by division; there are will and reason, succession of time and unmoving eternity, infinite change and ineffable rest!—

"Return Alpheus! the dread voice is past
Which shrunk thy streams!"
———"Thou honour'd flood,
Smooth-flowing Avon, crown'd with vocal reeds,
That strain I heard, was of a higher mood!—

But now my voice proceeds."

We may divide a dramatic poet's characteristics before we enter into the component merits of any one work, and with reference only to those things which are to be the materials of all, into language, passion, and character; always bearing in mind that these must act and react on each other,—the language inspired by the passion, and the language and the passion modified and differenced by the character. To the production of the highest excellencies in these three, there are requisite in the mind of the author;—good sense, talent, sensibility, imagination;—and to the perfection of a work we should add two faculties of lesser importance, yet necessary for the ornaments and foliage of the column and the roof—fancy and a quick sense of beauty.

As to language;—it cannot be supposed that the poet should make his characters say all that they would, or that, his whole drama considered, each scene, or paragraph should be such as, on cool examination, we can conceive it likely that men in such situations would say, in that order, or with that perfection. And yet, according to my feelings, it is a very inferior kind of poetry, in which, as in the French tragedies, men are made to talk in a style which few indeed even of the wittiest can be supposed to converse in, and which both is, and on a moment's reflection appears to be, the natural produce of the hot-bed of vanity, namely, the closet of an author, who is actuated originally by a desire to excite surprise and wonderment at his own superiority to other men,—instead of having felt so deeply on certain subjects, or in consequence of certain imaginations, as to make it almost a necessity of his nature to seek for sympathy,—no doubt, with that honourable desire of permanent action, which distinguishes genius.—Where then is the difference?—In this that each part should be proportionate, though the whole may be perhaps, impossible. At all events, it should be compatible with sound sense and logic in the mind of the poet himself.

It is to be lamented that we judge of books by books, instead of referring what we read to our own experience. One great use of books is to make their contents a motive for observation. The German tragedies have in some respects been justly ridiculed. In them the dramatist often becomes a novelist in his directions to the actors, and thus degrades tragedy into pantomime. Yet still the consciousness of the poet's mind must be diffused over that of the reader or spectator; but he himself, according to his genius, elevates us, and by being always in keeping, prevents us from perceiving any strangeness, though we feel great exultation. Many different kinds of style may be admirable, both in different men, and in different parts of the same poem.

See the different language which strong feelings may justify in Shylock, and learn from Shakespeare's conduct of that character the terrible force of every plain and calm diction, when known to proceed from a resolved and impassioned man.

It is especially with reference to the drama, and its characteristics in any given nation, or at any particular period, that the dependence of genius on the public taste becomes a matter of the deepest importance. I do not mean that taste which springs merely from caprice or fashionable imitation, and which, in fact, genius can, and by degrees will, create for itself; but that which arises out of wide-grasping and heart-enrooted causes, which is epidemic, and in the very air that all breathe. This it is which kills, or withers, or corrupts. Socrates, indeed, might walk arm in arm with Hygeia, whilst pestilence, with a thousand furies running to and fro, and clashing against each other in a complexity and agglomeration of horrors, was shooting her darts of fire and venom all around him. Even such was Milton; yea, and such, in spite of all that has been babbled by his critics in pretended excuse for his damning, because for them too profound excellencies,—such was Shakespeare. But alas!

the exceptions prove the rule. For who will dare to force his way out of the crowd,—not of the mere vulgar,—but of the vain and banded aristocracy of intellect, and presume to join the almost supernatural beings that stand by themselves aloof?

Of this diseased epidemic influence there are two forms especially preclusive of tragic worth. The first is the necessary growth of a sense and love of the ludicrous, and a morbid sensibility of the assimilative power,—an inflammation produced by cold and weakness,—which in the boldest bursts of passion will lie in wait for a jeer at any phrase, that may have an accidental coincidence in the mere words with something base or trivial. For instance,—to express woods, not on a plain, but clothing a hill, which overlooks a valley, or dell, or river, or the sea,—the trees rising one above another, as the spectators in an ancient theatre,—I know no other word in our language (bookish and pedantic terms out of the question), but hanging woods, the sylvæ superimpendentes of Catullus; yet let some wit call out in a slang tone,—"the gallows!" and a peal of laughter would damn the play. Hence it is that so many dull pieces have had a decent run, only because nothing unusual above, or absurd below, mediocrity furnished an occasion,—a spark for the explosive materials collected behind the orchestra. But it would take a volume of no ordinary size, however laconically the sense were expressed, if it were meant to instance the effects, and unfold all the causes, of this disposition upon the moral, intellectual, and even physical character of a people, with its influences on domestic life and individual deportment. A good document upon this subject would be the history of Paris society and of French, that is, Parisian, literature from the commencement of the latter half of the reign of Louis XIV. to that of Buonaparte, compared with the preceding philosophy and poetry even of Frenchmen themselves.

The second form, or more properly, perhaps, another distinct cause, of this diseased disposition is matter of exultation to the philanthropist and philosopher, and of regret to the poet, the painter, and the statuary alone, and to them only as poets, painters, and statuaries;—namely, the security, the comparative equability, and ever increasing sameness of human life. Men are now so seldom thrown into wild circumstances, and violences of excitement, that the language of such states, the laws of association of feeling with thought, the starts and strange far-flights of the assimilative power on the slightest and least obvious likeness presented by thoughts, words, or objects,—these are all judged of by authority, not by actual experience,—by what men have been accustomed to regard as symbols of these states, and not the natural symbols, or self-manifestations of them.

Even so it is in the language of man, and in that of nature. The sound sun, or the figures s, u, n, are purely arbitrary modes of recalling the object, and for visual mere objects they are not only sufficient, but have infinite advantages from their very nothingness per se. But the language of nature is a subordinate Logos, that was in the beginning, and was with the thing it represented, and was the thing it represented.

Now the language of Shakespeare, in his Lear for instance, is a something intermediate between these two; or rather it is the former blended with the latter,—the arbitrary, not merely recalling the cold notion of the thing, but expressing the reality of it, and, as arbitrary language is an heir-loom of the human race, being itself a part of that which it manifests. What shall I deduce from the preceding positions? Even this,—the appropriate, the never to be too much valued advantage of the theatre, if only the actors were what we know they have been,—a delightful, yet most effectual remedy for this dead palsy of the public mind. What would appear mad or ludicrous in a book, when presented to the senses under the form of reality, and with the truth of nature, supplies a species of actual experience. This is indeed the special privilege of a great actor over a great poet. No part was ever played in perfection, but nature justified herself in the hearts of all her children, in what state soever they were, short of absolute moral exhaustion, or downright stupidity. There is no time given to ask questions, or to pass judgments; we are taken by storm, and, though in the histrionic art many a clumsy counterfeit, by caricature of one or two features, may gain applause as a fine likeness, yet never was the very thing rejected as a counterfeit. O! when I think of the inexhaustible mine of virgin treasure in our Shakespeare, that I have been almost daily reading him since I was ten years old,—that the thirty intervening years have been unintermittingly and not fruitlessly employed in the study of the Greek, Latin, English, Italian, Spanish, and German belle lettrists, and the last fifteen years in addition, far more intensely in the analysis of the laws of life and reason as they exist in man,—and that upon every step I have made forward in taste, in acquisition of facts from history or my own observation, and in knowledge of the different laws of being and their apparent exceptions, from accidental collision of disturbing forces,—that at every new accession of information, after every successful exercise of meditation, and every fresh presentation of experience, I have unfailingly discovered a proportionate increase of wisdom and intuition in Shakespeare;—when I know this, and know too, that by a conceivable and possible, though hardly to be expected, arrangement of the British theatres, not all, indeed, but a large, a very large, proportion of this indefinite all—(round which no comprehension has yet drawn the line of circumscription, so as to say to itself, "I have seen the whole")—might be sent into the heads and hearts—into the very souls of the mass of mankind, to whom, except by this living comment and interpretation, it must remain for ever a sealed volume, a deep well without a wheel or a windlass;—it seems to me a pardonable enthusiasm to steal away from sober likelihood, and share in so rich a feast in the faery world of possibility! Yet even in the grave cheerfulness of a circumspect hope, much, very much, might be done; enough, assuredly, to furnish a kind and strenuous nature with ample motives for the attempt to effect what may be effected.

Shakespeare, A Poet Generally.

Clothed in radiant armour, and authorized by titles sure and manifold, as a poet, Shakespeare came forward to demand the throne of fame, as the dramatic poet of England. His excellences compelled even his contemporaries to seat him on that throne, although there were giants in those days contending for the same honour. Hereafter I would fain endeavour to make out the title of the English drama as created by, and existing in, Shakespeare, and its right to the supremacy of dramatic excellence in general. But he had shown himself a poet, previously to his appearance as a dramatic poet; and had no Lear, no Othello, no Henry IV., no Twelfth Night ever appeared, we must have admitted that Shakespeare possessed the chief, if not every, requisite of a poet,—deep feeling and exquisite sense of beauty, both as exhibited to the eye in the combinations of form, and to the ear in sweet and appropriate melody; that these feelings were under the command of his own will; that in his very first productions he projected his mind out of his own particular being, and felt, and made others feel, on subjects no way connected with himself, except by force of contemplation and that sublime faculty by which a great mind becomes that on which it meditates. To this must be added that affectionate love of nature and natural objects, without which no man could have observed so steadily, or painted so truly and passionately, the very minutest beauties of the external world:—

"And when thou hast on foot the purblind hare,
Mark the poor wretch; to overshoot his troubles,
How he outruns the wind, and with what care,
He cranks and crosses with a thousand doubles;

The many musits through the which he goes
Are like a labyrinth to amaze his foes.
"Sometimes he runs among the flock of sheep,
To make the cunning hounds mistake their smell;
And sometime where earth-delving conies keep,
To stop the loud pursuers in their yell;
And sometime sorteth with the herd of deer:
Danger deviseth shifts, wit waits on fear.
"For there his smell with others' being mingled,
The hot scent-snuffing hounds are driven to doubt,
Ceasing their clamorous cry, till they have singled
With much ado, the cold fault cleanly out,
Then do they spend their mouths; echo replies,
As if another chase were in the skies.
"By this poor Wat far off, upon a hill,
Stands on his hinder legs with listening ear,
To harken if his foes pursue him still:
Anon their loud alarums he doth hear,
And now his grief may be compared well
To one sore-sick, that hears the passing bell.
"Then shalt thou see the dew-bedabbled wretch
Turn, and return, indenting with the way:
Each envious briar his weary legs doth scratch,
Each shadow makes him stop, each murmur stay.
For misery is trodden on by many,
And being low, never relieved by any."
Venus and Adonis.
And the preceding description:—

"But lo! from forth a copse that neighbours by,
A breeding jennet, lusty, young and proud," &c.
is much more admirable, but in parts less fitted for quotation.

Moreover Shakespeare had shown that he possessed fancy, considered as the faculty of bringing together images dissimilar in the main by some one point or more of likeness, as in such a passage as this:—

"Full gently now she takes him by the hand,
A lily prisoned in a jail of snow,
Or ivory in an alabaster band:
So white a friend ingirts so white a foe!"—Ib.
And still mounting the intellectual ladder, he had as unequivocally proved the indwelling in his mind of imagination, or the power by which one image or feeling is made to modify many others, and by a sort of fusion to force many into one;—that which afterwards showed itself in such might and energy in Lear, where the deep anguish of a father spreads the feeling of ingratitude and cruelty over the very elements of heaven;—and which, combining many circumstances into one moment of consciousness, tends to produce that ultimate end of all human thought and human feeling, unity, and thereby the reduction of the spirit to its principle and fountain, who is alone truly one. Various are the workings of this the greatest faculty of the human mind, both passionate and tranquil. In its tranquil and purely pleasurable operation, it acts chiefly by creating out of many things, as they would have appeared in the description of an ordinary mind, detailed in unimpassioned succession,

a oneness, even as nature, the greatest of poets, acts upon us, when we open our eyes upon an extended prospect. Thus the flight of Adonis in the dusk of the evening:—

"Look! how a bright star shooteth from the sky;
So glides he in the night from Venus' eye!"

How many images and feelings are here brought together without effort and without discord, in the beauty of Adonis, the rapidity of his flight, the yearning, yet hopelessness, of the enamoured gazer, while a shadowy ideal character is thrown over the whole! Or this power acts by impressing the stamp of humanity, and of human feelings, on inanimate or mere natural objects:—

"Lo! here the gentle lark, weary of rest,
From his moist cabinet mounts up on high,
And wakes the morning, from whose silver breast
The sun ariseth in his majesty,
Who doth the world so gloriously behold,
The cedar-tops and hills seem burnish'd gold."

Or again, it acts by so carrying on the eye of the reader as to make him almost lose the consciousness of words,—to make him see every thing flashed, as Wordsworth has grandly and appropriately said:—

"Flashed upon the inward eye
Which is the bliss of solitude;"—

and this without exciting any painful or laborious attention, without any anatomy of description (a fault not uncommon in descriptive poetry),—but with the sweetness and easy movement of nature. This energy is an absolute essential of poetry, and of itself would constitute a poet, though not one of the highest class;—it is, however, a most hopeful symptom, and the Venus and Adonis is one continued specimen of it.

In this beautiful poem there is an endless activity of thought in all the possible associations of thought with thought, thought with feeling, or with words, of feelings with feelings, and of words with words.

"Even as the sun, with purple-colour'd face,
Had ta'en his last leave of the weeping morn,
Rose-cheek'd Adonis hied him to the chase:
Hunting he loved, but love he laughed to scorn.
Sick-thoughted Venus makes amain unto him,
And like a bold-faced suitor 'gins to woo him."

Remark the humanizing imagery and circumstances of the first two lines, and the activity of thought in the play of words in the fourth line. The whole stanza presents at once the time, the appearance of the morning, and the two persons distinctly characterised, and in six simple lines puts the reader in possession of the whole argument of the poem.

"Over one arm the lusty courser's rein,
Under the other was the tender boy,
Who blush'd and pouted in a dull disdain,
With leaden appetite, unapt to toy,
She red and hot, as coals of glowing fire,
He red for shame, but frosty to desire:"—

This stanza and the two following afford good instances of that poetic power, which I mentioned above, of making every thing present to the imagination—both the forms, and the passions which modify those forms, either actually, as in the representations of love or anger, or other human affections; or imaginatively, by the different manner in which inanimate objects, or objects unimpassioned themselves, are caused to be seen by the mind in moments of strong excitement, and according to the kind of the excitement,—whether of jealousy, or rage, or love, in the only appropriate sense of the word, or of the lower impulses of our nature, or finally of the poetic feeling itself. It is, perhaps, chiefly in the power of producing and reproducing the latter that the poet stands distinct.

The subject of the Venus and Adonis is unpleasing; but the poem itself is for that very reason the more illustrative of Shakespeare. There are men who can write passages of deepest pathos and even sublimity on circumstances personal to themselves and stimulative of their own passions; but they are not, therefore, on this account poets. Read that magnificent burst of woman's patriotism and exultation, Deborah's Song of Victory; it is glorious, but nature is the poet there. It is quite another matter to become all things and yet remain the same,—to make the changeful god be felt in the river, the lion, and the flame;—this it is, that is the true imagination. Shakespeare writes in this poem, as if he were of another planet, charming you to gaze on the movements of Venus and Adonis, as you would on the twinkling dances of two vernal butterflies.

Finally, in this poem and the Rape of Lucrece, Shakespeare gave ample proof of his possession of a most profound, energetic, and philosophical mind, without which he might have pleased, but could not have been a great dramatic poet. Chance and the necessity of his genius combined to lead him to the drama his proper province: in his conquest of which we should consider both the difficulties which opposed him, and the advantages by which he was assisted.

Shakespeare's Judgment equal to his Genius.

Thus then Shakespeare appears, from his Venus and Adonis and Rape of Lucrece alone, apart from all his great works, to have possessed all the conditions of the true poet. Let me now proceed to destroy, as far as may be in my power, the popular notion that he was a great dramatist by mere instinct, that he grew immortal in his own despite, and sank below men of second or third rate power, when he attempted aught beside the drama—even as bees construct their cells and manufacture their honey to admirable perfection; but would in vain attempt to build a nest. Now this mode of reconciling a compelled sense of inferiority with a feeling of pride, began in a few pedants, who having read that Sophocles was the great model of tragedy, and Aristotle the infallible dictator of its rules, and finding that the Lear, Hamlet, Othello and other master-pieces were neither in imitation of Sophocles, nor in obedience to Aristotle,—and not having (with one or two exceptions) the courage to affirm, that the delight which their country received from generation to generation, in defiance of the alterations of circumstances and habits, was wholly groundless,—took upon them, as a happy medium and refuge, to talk of Shakespeare as a sort of beautiful lusus naturæ, a delightful monster,—wild, indeed, and without taste or judgment, but like the inspired idiots so much venerated in the East, uttering, amid the strangest follies, the sublimest truths. In nine places out of ten in which I find his awful name mentioned, it is with some epithet of "wild," "irregular," "pure child of nature," &c. If all this be true, we must submit to it; though to a thinking mind it cannot but be painful to find any excellence, merely human, thrown out of all human analogy, and thereby leaving us neither rules for imitation, nor motives to imitate;—but if false, it is a dangerous falsehood;—for it affords a refuge to secret self-conceit,—enables a vain man at once to escape his reader's indignation by general swoln panegyrics, and merely by his ipse dixit to treat, as contemptible, what he has not intellect enough to comprehend, or soul to feel, without assigning any reason, or referring his opinion to any demonstrative principle;—thus leaving Shakespeare as a sort of grand Lama, adored indeed, and his very excrements prized as relics, but with no authority or real influence. I grieve that every late voluminous edition of his works would enable me to substantiate the present charge with a variety of facts, one-tenth of which would of themselves exhaust the time allotted to me. Every critic, who has or has not made a collection of black letter books—in itself a useful and respectable amusement,—puts on the seven-league boots of self-opinion, and strides at once from an illustrator into a supreme judge, and blind and deaf, fills his three-ounce phial at the waters of Niagara; and determines positively the greatness of the cataract to be neither more nor less than his three-ounce phial has been able to receive.

I think this a very serious subject. It is my earnest desire—my passionate endeavour—to enforce at various times and by various arguments and instances the close and reciprocal connection of just taste with pure morality. Without that acquaintance with the heart of man, or that docility and childlike gladness to be made acquainted with it, which those only can have, who dare look at their own hearts—and that with a steadiness which religion only has the power of reconciling with sincere humility;—without this, and the modesty produced by it, I am deeply convinced that no man, however wide his erudition, however patient his antiquarian researches, can possibly understand, or be worthy of understanding, the writings of Shakespeare.

Assuredly that criticism of Shakespeare will alone be genial which is reverential. The Englishman who, without reverence—a proud and affectionate reverence—can utter the name of William Shakespeare, stands disqualified for the office of critic. He wants one at least of the very senses, the language of which he is to employ, and will discourse at best but as a blind man, while the whole harmonious creation of light and shade with all its subtle interchange of deepening and dissolving colours rises in silence to the silent fiat of the uprising Apollo. However inferior in ability I may be to some who have followed me, I own I am proud that I was the first in time who publicly demonstrated to the full extent of the position, that the supposed irregularity and extravagances of Shakespeare were the mere dreams of a pedantry that arraigned the eagle because it had not the dimensions of the swan. In all the successive courses of lectures delivered by me, since my first attempt at the Royal Institution, it has been, and it still remains, my object, to prove that in all points from the most important to the most minute, the judgment of Shakespeare is commensurate with his genius,—nay, that his genius reveals itself in his judgment, as in its most exalted form. And the more gladly do I recur to this subject from the clear conviction, that to judge aright, and with distinct consciousness of the grounds of our judgment, concerning the works of Shakespeare, implies the power and the means of judging rightly of all other works of intellect, those of abstract science alone excepted.

It is a painful truth, that not only individuals, but even whole nations, are ofttimes so enslaved to the habits of their education and immediate circumstances, as not to judge disinterestedly even on those subjects, the very pleasure arising from which consists in its disinterestedness, namely, on subjects of taste and polite literature. Instead of deciding concerning their own modes and customs by any rule of reason, nothing appears rational, becoming, or beautiful to them, but what coincides with the peculiarities of their education. In this narrow circle, individuals may attain to exquisite discrimination, as the French critics have done in their own literature; but a true critic can no more be such without placing himself on some central point, from which he may command the whole,—that is, some general rule, which, founded in reason, or the faculties common to all men, must therefore apply to each,—than an astronomer can explain the movements of the solar system without taking his stand in the sun. And let me remark, that this will not tend to produce despotism, but, on the contrary, true tolerance, in the critic. He will, indeed, require, as the spirit and substance of a work, something true in human nature itself, and independent of all circumstances; but in the mode of applying it, he will estimate genius and judgment according to the felicity with which the imperishable soul of intellect shall have adapted itself to the age, the place, and the existing manners. The error he will expose, lies in reversing this, and holding up the mere circumstances as perpetual to the utter neglect of the power which can alone animate them. For art cannot exist without, or apart from nature; and what has man of his own to give to his fellow man, but his own thoughts and feelings, and his observations, so far as they are modified by his own thoughts or feelings?

Let me, then, once more submit this question to minds emancipated alike from national, or party, or sectarian prejudice:—Are the plays of Shakespeare works of rude uncultivated genius, in which the splendour of the parts compensates, if aught can compensate, for the barbarous shapelessness and irregularity of the whole?—Or is the form equally admirable with the matter, and the judgment of the great poet not less deserving our wonder than his genius?—Or, again, to repeat the question in other words:—is Shakespeare a great dramatic poet on account only of those beauties and excellences which he possesses in common with the ancients, but with diminished claims to our love and honour to the full extent of his differences from them?—Or are these very differences additional proofs of poetic wisdom, at once results and symbols of living power as contrasted with lifeless mechanism—of free and rival originality as contradistinguished from servile imitation, or, more accurately, a blind copying of effects, instead of a true imitation of the essential principles?—Imagine not that I am about to oppose genius to rules. No! the comparative value of these rules is the very cause to be tried. The spirit of poetry, like all other living powers, must of necessity circumscribe itself by rules, were it only to unite power with beauty. It must embody in order to reveal itself; but a living body is of necessity an organized one; and what is organization but the connection of parts in and for a whole, so that each part is at once end and means?—This is no discovery of criticism;—it is a necessity of the human mind; and all nations have felt and obeyed it, in the invention of metre, and measured sounds, as the vehicle and involucrum of poetry—itself a fellow-growth from the same life,—even as the bark is to the tree!

No work of true genius dares want its appropriate form, neither indeed is there any danger of this. As it must not, so genius cannot, be lawless; for it is even this that constitutes it genius—the power of acting creatively under laws of its own origination. How then comes it that not only single Zoili, but whole nations have combined in unhesitating condemnation of our great dramatist, as a sort of African nature, rich in beautiful monsters—as a wild heath where islands of fertility look the greener from the surrounding waste, where the loveliest plants now shine out among unsightly weeds, and now are choked by their parasitic growth, so intertwined that we cannot disentangle the weed without snapping the flower?—In this statement I have had no reference to the vulgar abuse of Voltaire, save as far as his charges are coincident with the decisions of Shakespeare's own commentators and (so they would tell you) almost idolatrous admirers. The true ground of the mistake lies in the confounding mechanical regularity with organic form. The form is mechanic, when on any given material we impress a pre-determined form, not necessarily arising out of the properties of the material;—as when to a mass of wet clay we give whatever shape we wish it to retain when hardened. The organic form, on the other hand is innate; it shapes, as it develops, itself from within, and the fulness of its development is one and the same with the perfection of its outward form. Such as the life is, such is the form. Nature, the prime genial artist, inexhaustible in diverse powers, is equally inexhaustible in forms;—each exterior is the physiognomy of the being within,—its true image reflected and thrown out from the concave mirror;—and even such is the appropriate excellence of her chosen poet, of our own Shakespeare,—himself a nature humanized, a genial understanding directing self-consciously a power and an implicit wisdom deeper even than our consciousness.

I greatly dislike beauties and selections in general; but as proof positive of his unrivalled excellence, I should like to try Shakespeare by this criterion. Make out your amplest catalogue of all the human faculties, as reason or the moral law, the will, the feeling of the coincidence of the two (a feeling sui generis et demonstratio demonstrationum) called the conscience, the understanding or prudence, wit, fancy, imagination, judgment,—and then of the objects on which these are to be employed, as the beauties, the terrors, and the seeming caprices of nature, the realities and the capabilities, that is, the actual and the ideal, of the human mind, conceived as an individual or as a social being, as in innocence or in guilt, in a play-paradise, or in a war-field of temptation;—and then compare with Shakespeare under each of these heads all or any of the writers in prose and verse that have ever lived! Who, that is competent to judge, doubts the result?—And ask your own hearts—ask your own common-sense—to conceive the possibility of this man being—I say not, the drunken savage of that wretched sciolist, whom Frenchmen, to their shame, have honoured before their elder and better worthies,—but the anomalous, the wild, the irregular, genius of our daily criticism! What! are we to have miracles in sport?—Or, I speak reverently, does God choose idiots by whom to convey divine truths to man?

Recapitulation, And Summary Of the Characteristics of Shakespeare's Dramas.

In lectures, of which amusement forms a large part of the object, there are some peculiar difficulties. The architect places his foundation out of sight, and the musician tunes his instrument before he makes his appearance; but the lecturer has to try his chords in the presence of the assembly; an operation not likely, indeed, to produce much pleasure, but yet indispensably necessary to a right understanding of the subject to be developed.

Poetry in essence is as familiar to barbarous as to civilized nations. The Laplander and the savage Indian are cheered by it as well as the inhabitants of London and Paris;—its spirit takes up and incorporates surrounding materials, as a plant clothes itself with soil and climate, whilst it exhibits the working of a vital principle within independent of all accidental circumstances. And to judge with fairness of an author's works, we ought to distinguish what is inward and essential from what is outward and circumstantial. It is essential to poetry that it be simple, and appeal to the elements and primary laws of our nature; that it be sensuous, and by its imagery elicit truth at a flash; that it be impassioned, and be able to move our feelings and awaken our affections. In comparing different poets with each other, we should inquire which have brought into the fullest play our imagination and our reason, or have created the greatest excitement and produced the completest harmony. If we consider great exquisiteness of language and sweetness of metre alone, it is impossible to deny to Pope the character of a delightful writer; but whether he be a poet, must depend upon our definition of the word; and, doubtless, if everything that pleases be poetry, Pope's satires and epistles must be poetry. This, I must say, that poetry, as distinguished from other modes of composition, does not rest in metre, and that it is not poetry, if it make no appeal to our passions or our imagination. One character belongs to all true poets, that they write from a principle within, not originating in any thing without; and that the true poet's work in its form, its shapings, and its modifications, is distinguished from all other works that assume to belong to the class of poetry, as a natural from an artificial flower, or as the mimic garden of a child from an enamelled meadow. In the former the flowers are broken from their stems and stuck into the ground; they are beautiful to the eye and fragrant to the sense, but their colours soon fade, and their odour is transient as the smile of the planter;—while the meadow may be visited again and again with renewed delight; its beauty is innate in the soil, and its bloom is of the freshness of nature.

The next ground of critical judgment, and point of comparison, will be as to how far a given poet has been influenced by accidental circumstances. As a living poet must surely write, not for the ages past, but for that in which he lives, and those which are to follow, it is on the one hand natural that he should not violate, and on the other necessary that he should not depend on, the mere manners and modes of his day. See how little does Shakespeare leave us to regret that he was born in his particular age! The great æra in modern times was what is called the Restoration of Letters;—the ages preceding it are called the dark ages; but it would be more wise, perhaps, to call them the ages in which we were in the dark. It is usually overlooked that the supposed dark period was not universal, but partial and successive, or alternate; that the dark age of England was not the dark age of Italy, but that one country was in its light and vigour, whilst another was in its gloom and bondage. But no sooner had the Reformation sounded through Europe like the blast of an archangel's trumpet, than from king to peasant there arose an enthusiasm for knowledge; the discovery of a manuscript became the subject of an embassy; Erasmus read by moonlight, because he could not afford a torch, and begged a penny, not for the love of charity, but for the love of learning. The three great points of attention were religion, morals, and taste; men of genius, as well as men of learning, who in this age need to be so widely distinguished, then alike became copyists of the ancients; and this, indeed, was the only way by which the taste of mankind could be improved, or their understandings informed. Whilst Dante imagined himself a humble follower of Virgil, and Ariosto of Homer, they were both unconscious of that greater power working within them, which in many points carried them beyond their supposed originals. All great discoveries bear the stamp of the age in which they are made;—hence we perceive the effects of the purer religion of the moderns visible for the most part in their lives; and in reading their works we should not content ourselves with the mere narratives of events long since passed, but should learn to apply their maxims and conduct to ourselves.

Having intimated that times and manners lend their form and pressure to genius, let me once more draw a slight parallel between the ancient and modern stage,—the stages of Greece and of England. The Greeks were polytheists; their religion was local; almost the only object of all their knowledge, art, and taste, was their gods; and, accordingly, their productions were, if the expression may be allowed, statuesque, whilst those of the moderns are picturesque. The Greeks reared a structure, which, in its parts, and as a whole, filled the mind with the calm and elevated impression of perfect beauty, and symmetrical proportion. The moderns also produced a whole—a more striking whole; but it was by blending materials, and fusing the parts together. And as the Pantheon is to York Minster or Westminster Abbey, so is Sophocles compared with Shakespeare; in the one a completeness, a satisfaction, an excellence, on which the mind rests with complacency; in the other a multitude of interlaced materials, great and little, magnificent and mean, accompanied, indeed, with the sense of a falling short of perfection, and yet, at the same time, so promising of our social and individual progression, that we would not, if we could, exchange it for that repose of the mind which dwells on the forms of symmetry in the acquiescent admiration of grace. This general characteristic of the ancient and modern drama might be illustrated by a parallel of the ancient and modern music;—the one consisting of melody arising from a succession only of pleasing sounds,—the modern embracing harmony also, the result of combination, and the effect of a whole.

I have said, and I say it again, that great as was the genius of Shakespeare, his judgment was at least equal to it. Of this any one will be convinced, who attentively considers those points in which the dramas of Greece and England differ, from the dissimilitude of circumstances by which each was modified and influenced. The Greek stage had its origin in the ceremonies of a sacrifice, such as of the goat to Bacchus, whom we most erroneously regard as merely the jolly god of wine;—for among the ancients he was venerable, as the symbol of that power which acts without our consciousness in the vital energies of nature—the vinum mundi—as Apollo was that of the conscious agency of our intellectual being. The heroes of old, under the influences of this Bacchic enthusiasm, performed more than human actions; hence tales of the favourite champions soon passed into dialogue. On the Greek stage the chorus was always before the audience; the curtain was never dropped, as we should say; and change of place being therefore, in general, impossible, the absurd notion of condemning it merely as improbable in itself was never entertained by any one. If we can believe ourselves at Thebes in one act, we may believe ourselves at Athens in the next.

If a story lasts twenty-four hours or twenty-four years, it is equally improbable. There seems to be no just boundary but what the feelings prescribe. But on the Greek stage, where the same persons were perpetually before the audience, great judgment was necessary in venturing on any such change. The poets never, therefore, attempted to impose on the senses by bringing places to men, but they did bring men to places, as in the well-known instance in the Eumenides, where, during an evident retirement of the chorus from the orchestra, the scene is changed to Athens, and Orestes is first introduced in the temple of Minerva, and the chorus of Furies come in afterwards in pursuit of him.

In the Greek drama there were no formal divisions into scenes and acts; there were no means, therefore, of allowing for the necessary lapse of time between one part of the dialogue and another, and unity of time in a strict sense was, of course, impossible. To overcome that difficulty of accounting for time, which is effected on the modern stage by dropping a curtain, the judgment and great genius of the ancients supplied music and measured motion, and with the lyric ode filled up the vacuity. In the story of the Agamemnon of Æschylus, the capture of Troy is supposed to be announced by a fire lighted on the Asiatic shore, and the transmission of the signal by successive beacons to Mycenæ. The signal is first seen at the 21st line, and the herald from Troy itself enters at the 486th, and Agamemnon himself at the 783rd line. But the practical absurdity of this was not felt by the audience, who, in imagination stretched minutes into hours, while they listened to the lofty narrative odes of the chorus which almost entirely filled up the interspace. Another fact deserves attention here, namely, that regularly on the Greek stage a drama, or acted story, consisted in reality of three dramas, called together a trilogy, and performed consecutively in the course of one day. Now you may conceive a tragedy of Shakespeare's as a trilogy connected in one single representation. Divide Lear into three parts, and each would be a play with the ancients; or take the three Æschylean dramas of Agamemnon, and divide them into, or call them, as many acts, and they together would be one play. The first act would comprise the usurpation of Ægisthus, and the murder of Agamemnon; the second, the revenge of Orestes, and the murder of his mother; and the third, the penance and absolution of Orestes;—occupying a period of twenty-two years.

The stage in Shakespeare's time was a naked room with a blanket for a curtain; but he made it a field for monarchs. That law of unity, which has its foundations, not in the factitious necessity of custom, but in nature itself, the unity of feeling, is everywhere and at all times observed by Shakespeare in his plays. Read Romeo and Juliet;—all is youth and spring;—

youth with its follies, its virtues, its precipitancies;—spring with its odours, its flowers, and its transiency; it is one and the same feeling that commences, goes through, and ends the play. The old men, the Capulets and Montagues, are not common old men; they have an eagerness, a heartiness, a vehemence, the effect of spring; with Romeo, his change of passion, his sudden marriage, and his rash death, are all the effects of youth;—whilst in Juliet love has all that is tender and melancholy in the nightingale, all that is voluptuous in the rose, with whatever is sweet in the freshness of spring; but it ends with a long deep sigh like the last breeze of the Italian evening. This unity of feeling and character pervades every drama of Shakespeare.

It seems to me that his plays are distinguished from those of all other dramatic poets by the following characteristics:—

1. Expectation in preference to surprise. It is like the true reading of the passage—"God said, Let there be light, and there was light;"—not, there was light. As the feeling with which we startle at a shooting star compared with that of watching the sunrise at the pre-established moment, such and so low is surprise compared with expectation.

2. Signal adherence to the great law of nature, that all opposites tend to attract and temper each other. Passion in Shakespeare generally displays libertinism, but involves morality; and if there are exceptions to this, they are, independently of their intrinsic value, all of them indicative of individual character, and, like the farewell admonitions of a parent, have an end beyond the parental relation. Thus the Countess's beautiful precepts to Bertram, by elevating her character, raise that of Helena her favourite, and soften down the point in her which Shakespeare does not mean us not to see, but to see and to forgive, and at length to justify. And so it is in Polonius, who is the personified memory of wisdom no longer actually possessed. This admirable character is always misrepresented on the stage. Shakespeare never intended to exhibit him as a buffoon; for although it was natural that Hamlet—a young man of fire and genius, detesting formality, and disliking Polonius on political grounds, as imagining that he had assisted his uncle in his usurpation—should express himself satirically, yet this must not be taken as exactly the poet's conception of him. In Polonius a certain induration of character had arisen from long habits of business; but take his advice to Laertes, and Ophelia's reverence for his memory, and we shall see that he was meant to be represented as a statesman somewhat past his faculties,—his recollections of life all full of wisdom, and showing a knowledge of human nature, whilst what immediately takes place before him, and escapes from him, is indicative of weakness.

But as in Homer all the deities are in armour, even Venus; so in Shakespeare all the characters are strong. Hence real folly and dulness are made by him the vehicles of wisdom. There is no difficulty for one being a fool to imitate a fool; but to be, remain, and speak like a wise man and a great wit, and yet so as to give a vivid representation of a veritable fool,—hic labor, hoc opus est. A drunken constable is not uncommon, nor hard to draw; but see and examine what goes to make up a Dogberry.

3. Keeping at all times in the high road of life. Shakespeare has no innocent adulteries, no interesting incests, no virtuous vice;—he never renders that amiable which religion and reason alike teach us to detest, or clothes impurity in the garb of virtue, like Beaumont and Fletcher, the Kotzebues of the day. Shakespeare's fathers are roused by ingratitude, his husbands stung by unfaithfulness; in him, in short, the affections are wounded in those points in which all may, nay, must, feel. Let the morality of Shakespeare be contrasted with that of the writers of his own, or the succeeding age, or of those of the present day, who boast their superiority in this respect. No one can dispute that the result of such a

comparison is altogether in favour of Shakespeare;—even the letters of women of high rank in his age were often coarser than his writings. If he occasionally disgusts a keen sense of delicacy, he never injures the mind; he neither excites, nor flatters, passion, in order to degrade the subject of it; he does not use the faulty thing for a faulty purpose, nor carries on warfare against virtue, by causing wickedness to appear as no wickedness, through the medium of a morbid sympathy with the unfortunate. In Shakespeare vice never walks as in twilight; nothing is purposely out of its place;—he inverts not the order of nature and propriety,—does not make every magistrate a drunkard or glutton, nor every poor man meek, humane, and temperate; he has no benevolent butchers, nor any sentimental rat-catchers.

4. Independence of the dramatic interest on the plot. The interest in the plot is always in fact on account of the characters, not vice versa, as in almost all other writers; the plot is a mere canvass and no more. Hence arises the true justification of the same stratagem being used in regard to Benedict and Beatrice,—the vanity in each being alike. Take away from the Much Ado about Nothing all that which is not indispensable to the plot, either as having little to do with it, or, at best, like Dogberry and his comrades, forced into the service, when any other less ingeniously absurd watchmen and night-constables would have answered the mere necessities of the action;—take away Benedict, Beatrice, Dogberry, and the reaction of the former on the character of Hero,—and what will remain? In other writers the main agent of the plot is always the prominent character; in Shakespeare it is so, or is not so, as the character is in itself calculated, or not calculated, to form the plot. Don John is the main-spring of the plot of this play; but he is merely shown and then withdrawn.

5. Independence of the interest on the story as the ground-work of the plot. Hence Shakespeare never took the trouble of inventing stories. It was enough for him to select from those that had been already invented or recorded such as had one or other, or both, of two recommendations, namely, suitableness to his particular purpose, and their being parts of popular tradition,—names of which we had often heard, and of their fortunes, and as to which all we wanted was, to see the man himself. So it is just the man himself—the Lear, the Shylock, the Richard—that Shakespeare makes us for the first time acquainted with. Omit the first scene in Lear, and yet everything will remain; so the first and second scenes in the Merchant of Venice. Indeed it is universally true.

6. Interfusion of the lyrical—that which in its very essence is poetical—not only with the dramatic, as in the plays of Metastasio, where at the end of the scene comes the aria as the exit speech of the character,—but also in and through the dramatic. Songs in Shakespeare are introduced as songs only, just as songs are in real life, beautifully as some of them are characteristic of the person who has sung or called for them, as Desdemona's "Willow," and Ophelia's wild snatches, and the sweet carollings in As You Like It. But the whole of the Midsummer Night's Dream is one continued specimen of the dramatised lyrical. And observe how exquisitely the dramatic of Hotspur;—

"Marry, and I'm glad on't with all my heart;
I'd rather be a kitten and cry—mew." &c.
melts away into the lyric of Mortimer;—

"I understand thy looks: that pretty Welsh
Which thou pourest down from these swelling heavens,
I am too perfect in," &c.
Henry IV. part i. act iii, sc. 1.

7. The characters of the dramatis personæ, like those in real life, are to be inferred by the reader;—they are not told to him. And it is well worth remarking that Shakespeare's characters, like those in real life, are very commonly misunderstood, and almost always understood by different persons in different ways. The causes are the same in either case. If you take only what the friends of the character say, you may be deceived, and still more so, if that which his enemies say; nay, even the character himself sees himself through the medium of his character, and not exactly as he is. Take all together, not omitting a shrewd hint from the clown or the fool, and perhaps your impression will be right; and you may know whether you have in fact discovered the poet's own idea, by all the speeches receiving light from it, and attesting its reality by reflecting it.

Lastly, in Shakespeare the heterogeneous is united, as it is in nature. You must not suppose a pressure or passion always acting on or in the character!—passion in Shakespeare is that by which the individual is distinguished from others, not that which makes a different kind of him. Shakespeare followed the main march of the human affections. He entered into no analysis of the passions or faiths of men, but assured himself that such and such passions and faiths were grounded in our common nature, and not in the mere accidents of ignorance or disease. This is an important consideration, and constitutes our Shakespeare the morning star, the guide and the pioneer, of true philosophy.

Outline Of An Introductory Lecture Upon Shakespeare.

Of that species of writing termed tragi-comedy, much has been produced and doomed to the shelf. Shakespeare's comic are continually reacting upon his tragic characters. Lear, wandering amidst the tempest, has all his feelings of distress increased by the overflowings of the wild wit of the Fool, as vinegar poured upon wounds exacerbates their pain. Thus, even his comic humour tends to the development of tragic passion.

The next characteristic of Shakespeare is his keeping at all times in the high road of life, &c. Another evidence of his exquisite judgment is, that he seizes hold of popular tales; Lear and the Merchant of Venice were popular tales, but are so excellently managed, that both are the representations of men in all countries and of all times.

His dramas do not arise absolutely out of some one extraordinary circumstance, the scenes may stand independently of any such one connecting incident, as faithful representations of men and manners. In his mode of drawing characters there are no pompous descriptions of a man by himself; his character is to be drawn, as in real life, from the whole course of the play, or out of the mouths of his enemies or friends. This may be exemplified in Polonius, whose character has been often misrepresented. Shakespeare never intended him for a buffoon, &c.

Another excellence of Shakespeare, in which no writer equals him, is in the language of nature. So correct is it, that we can see ourselves in every page. The style and manner have also that felicity, that not a sentence can be read, without its being discovered if it is Shakespearian. In observation of living characters—of landlords and postilions—Fielding has great excellence; but in drawing from his own heart, and depicting that species of character, which no observation could teach, he failed in comparison with Richardson, who perpetually places himself, as it were, in a day-dream. Shakespeare excels in both. Witness the accuracy of character in Juliet's name; while for the great characters of Iago, Othello, Hamlet, Richard III., to which he could never have seen anything similar, he seems invariably to have asked himself—How should I act or speak in such circumstances? His comic characters are also peculiar. A drunken constable was not uncommon; but he makes folly a vehicle for wit, as in Dogberry: everything is a sub-stratum on which his genius can erect the mightiest superstructure.

To distinguish that which is legitimate in Shakespeare from what does not belong to him, we must observe his varied images symbolical of novel truth, thrusting by, and seeming to trip up each other, from an impetuosity of thought, producing a flowing metre, and seldom closing with the line. In Pericles, a play written fifty years before, but altered by Shakespeare, his additions may be recognised to half a line, from the metre, which has the same perfection in the flowing continuity of interchangeable metrical pauses in his earliest plays, as in Love's Labour's Lost.

Lastly, contrast his morality with the writers of his own or of the succeeding age, &c. If a man speak injuriously of our friend, our vindication of him is naturally warm. Shakespeare has been accused of profaneness. I for my part have acquired from perusal of him, a habit of looking into my own heart, and am confident that Shakespeare is an author of all others the most calculated to make his readers better as well as wiser.

Shakespeare, possessed of wit, humour, fancy, and imagination, built up an outward world from the stores within his mind, as the bee finds a hive from a thousand sweets gathered from a thousand flowers. He was not only a great poet but a great philosopher. Richard III., Iago, and Falstaff are men who reverse the order of things, who place intellect at the head, whereas it ought to follow, like Geometry, to prove and to confirm. No man, either hero or saint, ever acted from an unmixed motive; for let him do what he will rightly, still Conscience whispers "it is your duty." Richard, laughing at conscience and sneering at religion, felt a confidence in his intellect, which urged him to commit the most horrid crimes, because he felt himself, although inferior in form and shape, superior to those around him; he felt he possessed a power which they had not. Iago, on the same principle, conscious of superior intellect, gave scope to his envy, and hesitated not to ruin a gallant, open, and generous friend in the moment of felicity, because he was not promoted as he expected. Othello was superior in place, but Iago felt him to be inferior in intellect, and, unrestrained by conscience, trampled upon him. Falstaff, not a degraded man of genius, like Burns, but a man of degraded genius, with the same consciousness of superiority to his companions, fastened himself on a young Prince, to prove how much his influence on an heir-apparent would exceed that of a statesman. With this view he hesitated not to adopt the most contemptible of all characters, that of an open and professed liar: even his sensuality was subservient to his intellect: for he appeared to drink sack, that he might have occasion to show off his wit. One thing, however, worthy of observation, is the perpetual contrast of labour in Falstaff to produce wit, with the ease with which Prince Henry parries his shafts; and the final contempt which such a character deserves and receives from the young king, when Falstaff exhibits the struggle of inward determination with an outward show of humility.

Order Of Shakespeare's Plays.

Various attempts have been made to arrange the plays of Shakespeare, each according to its priority in time, by proofs derived from external documents. How unsuccessful these attempts have been might easily be shewn, not only from the widely different results arrived at by men, all deeply versed in the black-letter books, old plays, pamphlets, manuscript records, and catalogues of that age, but also from the fallacious and unsatisfactory nature of the facts and assumptions on which the evidence rests. In that age, when the press was chiefly occupied with controversial or practical divinity,—when the law, the Church, and the State engrossed all honour and respectability,—when a degree of disgrace, levior quædam infamiæ macula, was attached to the publication of poetry, and even to have sported with the Muse, as a private relaxation, was supposed to be—a venial fault, indeed, yet—something beneath the gravity of a wise man,—when the professed poets were so poor, that the very expenses of the press demanded the liberality of some wealthy individual, so that two-thirds of Spenser's poetic works, and those most highly praised by his learned admirers and friends, remained for many years in manuscript, and in manuscript perished,—when the amateurs of the stage were comparatively few, and therefore for the greater part more or less known to each other,—when we know that the plays of Shakespeare, both during and after his life, were the property of the stage, and published by the players, doubtless according to their notions of acceptability with the visitants of the theatre,—in such an age, and under such circumstances, can an allusion or reference to any drama or poem in the publication of a contemporary be received as conclusive evidence, that such drama or poem had at that time been published? Or, further, can the priority of publication itself prove anything in favour of actually prior composition?

We are tolerably certain, indeed, that the Venus and Adonis, and the Rape of Lucrece, were his two earliest poems, and though not printed until 1593, in the twenty-ninth year of his age, yet there can be little doubt that they had remained by him in manuscript many years. For Mr. Malone has made it highly probable that he had commenced as a writer for the stage in 1591, when he was twenty-seven years old, and Shakespeare himself assures us that the Venus and Adonis was the first heir of his invention.

Baffled, then, in the attempt to derive any satisfaction from outward documents, we may easily stand excused if we turn our researches towards the internal evidences furnished by the writings themselves, with no other positive data than the known facts that the Venus and Adonis was printed in 1593, the Rape of Lucrece in 1594, and that the Romeo and Juliet had appeared in 1595,—and with no other presumptions than that the poems, his very first productions, were written many years earlier—(for who can believe that Shakespeare could have remained to his twenty-ninth or thirtieth year without attempting poetic composition of any kind?),—and that between these and Romeo and Juliet there had intervened one or two other dramas, or the chief materials, at least of them, although they may very possibly have appeared after the success of the Romeo and Juliet, and some other circumstances, had given the poet an authority with the proprietors, and created a prepossession in his favour with the theatrical audiences.

CLASSIFICATION ATTEMPTED, 1802.

FIRST EPOCH.

The London Prodigal.
Cromwell.
Henry VI., three parts, first edition.
The old King John.
Edward III.
The old Taming of the Shrew.
Pericles.
All these are transition works, Uebergangswerke; not his, yet of him.

SECOND EPOCH.

All's Well that Ends Well;—but afterwards worked up afresh (umgearbeitet), especially Parolles.
The Two Gentlemen of Verona; a sketch.
Romeo and Juliet; first draft of it.

THIRD EPOCH

rises into the full, although youthful, Shakespeare; it was the negative period of his perfection.

Love's Labour's Lost.
Twelfth Night.
As You Like It.
Midsummer Night's Dream.
Richard II.
Henry IV. and V.
Henry VIII.; Gelegenheitsgedicht.
Romeo and Juliet, as at present.
Merchant of Venice.

FOURTH EPOCH.

Much Ado about Nothing.
Merry Wives of Windsor; first edition.
Henry VI.; rifacimento.

FIFTH EPOCH.

The period of beauty was now past; and that of δεινότης and grandeur succeeds.

Lear.
Macbeth.
Hamlet.
Timon of Athens; an after vibration of Hamlet.
Troilus and Cressida; Uebergang in die Ironie.
The Roman Plays.
King John, as at present.
Merry Wives of Windsor
Taming of the Shrew umgearbeitet.
Measure for Measure.
Othello.
Tempest.
Winter's Tale.
Cymbeline.

CLASSIFICATION ATTEMPTED, 1810.

Shakespeare's earliest dramas I take to be—

Love's Labour's Lost.
All's Well that Ends Well.
Comedy of Errors.
Romeo and Juliet.
In the second class I reckon—

Midsummer Night's Dream.
As You Like It.
Tempest.
Twelfth Night.
In the third, as indicating a greater energy—not merely of poetry, but of all the world of thought, yet still with some of the growing pains, and the awkwardness of growth—I place—

Troilus and Cressida.
Cymbeline.
Merchant of Venice.
Much Ado about Nothing.
Taming of the Shrew.
In the fourth, I place the plays containing the greatest characters—

Macbeth.
Lear.
Hamlet.
Othello.
And lastly, the historic dramas, in order to be able to show my reasons for rejecting some whole plays, and very many scenes in others.

CLASSIFICATION ATTEMPTED, 1819.

I think Shakespeare's earliest dramatic attempt—perhaps even prior in conception to the Venus and Adonis, and planned before he left Stratford—was Love's Labour's Lost. Shortly afterwards I suppose Pericles and certain scenes in Jeronymo to have been produced; and in the same epoch, I place the Winter's Tale and Cymbeline, differing from the Pericles by the entire rifacimento of it, when Shakespeare's celebrity as poet, and his interest, no less than his influence, as manager, enabled him to bring forward the laid-by labours of his youth. The example of Titus Andronicus, which, as well as Jeronymo, was most popular in Shakespeare's first epoch, had led the young dramatist to the lawless mixture of dates and manners. In this same epoch I should place the Comedy of Errors, remarkable as being the only specimen of poetical farce in our language, that is, intentionally such; so that all the distinct kinds of drama, which might be educed a priori, have their representatives in Shakespeare's works. I say intentionally such; for many of Beaumont and Fletcher's plays, and the greater part of Ben Jonson's comedies, are farce plots. I add All's Well that Ends Well, originally intended as the counterpart of Love's Labour's Lost, Taming of the Shrew, Midsummer Night's Dream, Much Ado about Nothing, and Romeo and Juliet.

SECOND EPOCH.

Richard II.
King John.

Henry VI.,—rifacimento only.
Richard III.

THIRD EPOCH.

Henry IV.
Henry V.
Merry Wives of Windsor.
Henry VIII.,—a sort of historical masque, or show play.

FOURTH EPOCH

gives all the graces and facilities of a genius in full possession and habitual exercise of power, and peculiarly of the feminine, the lady's character.

Tempest.
As You Like It
Merchant of Venice.
Twelfth Night.
And, finally, at its very point of culmination—

Lear.
Hamlet.
Macbeth.
Othello.

LAST EPOCH.

when the energies of intellect in the cycle of genius were, though in a rich and more potentiated form, becoming predominant over passion and creative self-manifestation—

Measure for Measure,
Timon of Athens.
Coriolanus.
Julius Cæsar.
Antony and Cleopatra.
Troilus and Cressida.
Merciful, wonder-making Heaven! what a man was this Shakespeare! Myriad-minded, indeed, he was.

Notes On The "Tempest."

There is a sort of improbability with which we are shocked in dramatic representation, not less than in a narrative of real life. Consequently, there must be rules respecting it; and as rules are nothing but means to an end previously ascertained—(inattention to which simple truth has been the occasion of all the pedantry of the French school),—we must first determine what the immediate end or object of the drama is. And here, as I have previously remarked, I find two extremes of critical decision;—the French, which evidently presupposes that a perfect delusion is to be aimed at,—an opinion which needs no fresh confutation; and the exact opposite to it, brought forward by Dr. Johnson, who supposes the auditors throughout in the full reflective knowledge of the contrary. In evincing the impossibility of delusion, he makes no sufficient allowance for an intermediate state, which I have before distinguished by the term illusion, and have attempted to illustrate its quality and character by reference to our mental state when dreaming. In both cases we simply do not judge the imagery to be unreal; there is a negative reality, and no more. Whatever, therefore, tends to prevent the mind from placing itself, or being placed, gradually in that state in which the images have such negative reality for the auditor, destroys this illusion, and is dramatically improbable.

Now, the production of this effect—a sense of improbability—will depend on the degree of excitement in which the mind is supposed to be. Many things would be intolerable in the first scene of a play, that would not at all interrupt our enjoyment in the height of the interest, when the narrow cockpit may be made to hold

"The vasty field of France, or we may cram
Within its wooden O, the very casques,
That did affright the air at Agincourt."

Again, on the other hand, many obvious improbabilities will be endured, as belonging to the groundwork of the story rather than to the drama itself, in the first scenes, which would disturb or disentrance us from all illusion in the acme of our excitement; as for instance, Lear's division of his kingdom, and the banishment of Cordelia.

But, although the other excellences of the drama besides this dramatic probability, as unity of interest, with distinctness and subordination of the characters, and appropriateness of style, are all, so far as they tend to increase the inward excitement, means towards accomplishing the chief end, that of producing and supporting this willing illusion,—yet they do not on that account cease to be ends themselves; and we must remember that, as such, they carry their own justification with them, as long as they do not contravene or interrupt the total illusion. It is not even always, or of necessity, an objection to them, that they prevent the illusion from rising to as great a height as it might otherwise have attained;—it is enough that they are simply compatible with as high a degree of it as is requisite for the purpose. Nay, upon particular occasions, a palpable improbability may be hazarded by a great genius for the express purpose of keeping down the interest of a merely instrumental scene, which would otherwise make too great an impression for the harmony of the entire illusion. Had the panorama been invented in the time of Pope Leo X., Raffael would still, I doubt not, have smiled in contempt at the regret, that the broom twigs and scrubby bushes at the back of some of his grand pictures were not as probable trees as those in the exhibition.

The Tempest is a specimen of the purely romantic drama, in which the interest is not historical, or dependent upon fidelity of portraiture, or the natural connection of events, but is a birth of the imagination, and rests only upon the coaptation and union of the elements granted to, or assumed by, the poet. It is a species of drama which owes no allegiance to time or space, and in which, therefore, errors of chronology and geography—no mortal sins in any species—are venial faults, and count for nothing. It addresses itself entirely to the imaginative faculty; and although the illusion may be assisted by the effect on the senses of the complicated scenery and decorations of modern times, yet this sort of assistance is dangerous. For the principal and only genuine excitement ought to come from within— from the moved and sympathetic imagination; whereas, where so much is addressed to the mere external senses of seeing and hearing, the spiritual vision is apt to languish, and the attraction from without will withdraw the mind from the proper and only legitimate interest which is intended to spring from within.

The romance opens with a busy scene admirably appropriate to the kind of drama, and giving, as it were, the key-note to the whole harmony. It prepares and initiates the excitement required for the entire piece, and yet does not demand anything from the spectators, which their previous habits had not fitted them to understand. It is the bustle of a tempest, from which the real horrors are abstracted;—therefore it is poetical, though not in strictness natural—(the distinction to which I have so often alluded)—and is purposely restrained from concentering the interest on itself, but used merely as an induction or tuning for what is to follow.

In the second scene, Prospero's speeches, till the entrance of Ariel, contain the finest example I remember of retrospective narration for the purpose of exciting immediate interest, and putting the audience in possession of all the information necessary for the understanding of the plot. Observe, too, the perfect probability of the moment chosen by Prospero (the very Shakespeare himself, as it were, of the tempest) to open out the truth to his daughter, his own romantic bearing, and how completely anything that might have been disagreeable to us in the magician, is reconciled and shaded in the humanity and natural feelings of the father. In the very first speech of Miranda, the simplicity and tenderness of her character are at once laid open;—it would have been lost in direct contact with the agitation of the first scene. The opinion once prevailed, but happily is now abandoned, that Fletcher alone wrote for women;—the truth is, that with very few, and those partial exceptions, the female characters in the plays of Beaumont and Fletcher are, when of the light kind, not decent; when heroic, complete viragos. But in Shakespeare all the elements of womanhood are holy, and there is the sweet yet dignified feeling of all that continuates society, as sense of ancestry and of sex, with a purity unassailable by sophistry, because it rests not in the analytic processes, but in that sane equipoise of the faculties, during which the feelings are representative of all past experience,—not of the individual only, but of all those by whom she has been educated, and their predecessors, even up to the first mother that lived. Shakespeare saw that the want of prominence, which Pope notices for sarcasm, was the blessed beauty of the woman's character, and knew that it arose not from any deficiency, but from the more exquisite harmony of all the parts of the moral being constituting one living total of head and heart. He has drawn it, indeed, in all its distinctive energies of faith, patience, constancy, fortitude,—shown in all of them as following the heart, which gives its results by a nice tact and happy intuition, without the intervention of the discursive faculty, sees all things in and by the light of the affections, and errs, if it ever err, in the exaggerations of love alone. In all the Shakespearian women there is essentially the same foundation and principle; the distinct individuality and variety are merely the result of modification of circumstances, whether in Miranda the maiden, in Imogen the wife, or in Katherine the queen.

But to return. The appearance and characters of the super or ultra natural servants are finely contrasted. Ariel has in everything the airy tint which gives the name; and it is worthy of remark that Miranda is never directly brought into comparison with Ariel, lest the natural and human of the one and the supernatural of the other should tend to neutralise each other; Caliban, on the other hand, is all earth, all condensed and gross in feelings and images; he has the dawnings of understanding without reason or the moral sense, and in him, as in some brute animals, this advance to the intellectual faculties, without the moral sense, is marked by the appearance of vice. For it is in the primacy of the moral being only that man is truly human; in his intellectual powers he is certainly approached by the brutes, and, man's whole system duly considered, those powers cannot be considered other than means to an end—that is, to morality.

In this scene, as it proceeds, is displayed the impression made by Ferdinand and Miranda on each other; it is love at first sight;—

... "At the first sight
They have chang'd eyes;"—
and it appears to me, that in all cases of real love, it is at one moment that it takes place. That moment may have been prepared by previous esteem, admiration, or even affection,—yet love seems to require a momentary act of volition, by which a tacit bond of devotion is imposed,—a bond not to be thereafter broken without violating what should be sacred in our nature. How finely is the true Shakespearian scene contrasted with Dryden's vulgar alteration of it, in which a mere ludicrous psychological experiment, as it were, is tried—displaying nothing but indelicacy without passion.

Prospero's interruption of the courtship has often seemed to me to have had no sufficient motive; still, his alleged reason—

... "Lest too light winning
Make the prize light"—
is enough for the ethereal connections of the romantic imagination, although it would not be so for the historical. The whole courting scene, indeed, in the beginning of the third act, between the lovers, is a masterpiece; and the first dawn of disobedience in the mind of Miranda to the command of her father is very finely drawn, so as to seem the working of the Scriptural command—"Thou shalt leave father and mother," &c. Oh! with what exquisite purity this scene is conceived and executed! Shakespeare may sometimes be gross, but I boldly say that he is always moral and modest. Alas! in this our day, decency of manners is preserved at the expense of morality of heart, and delicacies for vice are allowed, whilst grossness against it is hypocritically, or at least morbidly, condemned.

In this play are admirably sketched the vices generally accompanying a low degree of civilisation; and in the first scene of the second act Shakespeare has, as in many other places, shown the tendency in bad men to indulge in scorn and contemptuous expressions as a mode of getting rid of their own uneasy feelings of inferiority to the good, and also, by making the good ridiculous, of rendering the transition of others to wickedness easy. Shakespeare never puts habitual scorn into the mouths of other than bad men, as here in the instances of Antonio and Sebastian. The scene of the intended assassination of Alonzo and Gonzalo is an exact counterpart of the scene between Macbeth and his lady, only pitched in a lower key throughout, as designed to be frustrated and concealed, and exhibiting the same profound management in the manner of familiarising a mind, not immediately recipient, to the suggestion of guilt, by associating the proposed crime with something ludicrous or out of place,—something not habitually matter of reverence. By this kind of sophistry the imagination and fancy are first bribed to contemplate the suggested act, and at length to become acquainted with it. Observe how the effect of this scene is heightened by contrast with another counterpart of it in low life,—that between the conspirators Stephano, Caliban, and Trinculo in the second scene of the third act, in which there are the same essential characteristics.

In this play, and in this scene of it, are also shown the springs of the vulgar in politics,—of that kind of politics which is inwoven with human nature. In his treatment of this subject, wherever it occurs, Shakespeare is quite peculiar. In other writers we find the particular opinions of the individual; in Massinger it is rank republicanism; in Beaumont and Fletcher even jure divino principles are carried to excess;—but Shakespeare never promulgates any party tenets. He is always the philosopher and the moralist, but at the same time with a profound veneration for all the established institutions of society, and for those classes which form the permanent elements of the State,—especially never introducing a professional character, as such, otherwise than as respectable. If he must have any name, he should be styled a philosophical aristocrat, delighting in those hereditary institutions which have a tendency to bind one age to another, and in that distinction of ranks, of which, although few may be in possession, all enjoy the advantages. Hence, again, you will observe the good nature with which he seems always to make sport with the passions and follies of a mob, as with an irrational animal. He is never angry with it, but hugely content with holding up its absurdities to its face; and sometimes you may trace a tone of almost affectionate superiority, something like that in which a father speaks of the rogueries of a child. See the good-humoured way in which he describes Stephano passing from the most licentious freedom to absolute despotism over Trinculo and Caliban. The truth is, Shakespeare's characters are all genera intensely individualised; the results of meditation, of which observation supplied the drapery and the colours necessary to combine them with each other. He had virtually surveyed all the great component powers and impulses of human nature,—had seen that their different combinations and subordinations were in fact the individualisers of men, and showed how their harmony was produced by reciprocal disproportions of excess or deficiency. The language in which these truths are expressed was not drawn from any set fashion, but from the profoundest depths of his moral being, and is therefore for all ages.

"Love's Labour's Lost."

The characters in this play are either impersonated out of Shakespeare's own multiformity by imaginative self-position, or out of such as a country town and schoolboy's observation might supply,—the curate, the schoolmaster, the Armado (who even in my time was not extinct in the cheaper inns of North Wales), and so on. The satire is chiefly on follies of words. Biron and Rosaline are evidently the pre-existent state of Benedict and Beatrice, and so, perhaps, is Boyet of Lafeu, and Costard of the tapster in Measure for Measure; and the frequency of the rhymes, the sweetness as well as the smoothness of the metre, and the number of acute and fancifully illustrated aphorisms, are all as they ought to be in a poet's youth. True genius begins by generalising and condensing; it ends in realising and expanding. It first collects the seeds.

Yet, if this juvenile drama had been the only one extant of our Shakespeare, and we possessed the tradition only of his riper works, or accounts of them in writers who had not even mentioned this play,—how many of Shakespeare's characteristic features might we not still have discovered in Love's Labour's Lost, though as in a portrait taken of him in his boyhood.

I can never sufficiently admire the wonderful activity of thought throughout the whole of the first scene of the play, rendered natural, as it is, by the choice of the characters, and the whimsical determination on which the drama is founded. A whimsical determination certainly;—yet not altogether so very improbable to those who are conversant in the history of the middle ages, with their Courts of Love, and all that lighter drapery of chivalry, which engaged even mighty kings with a sort of serio-comic interest, and may well be supposed to have occupied more completely the smaller princes, at a time when the noble's or prince's court contained the only theatre of the domain or principality. This sort of story, too, was admirably suited to Shakespeare's times, when the English court was still the foster-mother of the state and the muses; and when, in consequence, the courtiers, and men of rank and fashion, affected a display of wit, point, and sententious observation, that would be deemed intolerable at present,—but in which a hundred years of controversy, involving every great political, and every dear domestic, interest, had trained all but the lowest classes to participate. Add to this the very style of the sermons of the time, and the eagerness of the Protestants to distinguish themselves by long and frequent preaching, and it will be found that, from the reign of Henry VIII. to the abdication of James II. no country ever received such a national education as England.

Hence the comic matter chosen in the first instance is a ridiculous imitation or apery of this constant striving after logical precision and subtle opposition of thoughts, together with a making the most of every conception or image, by expressing it under the least expected property belonging to it, and this, again, rendered specially absurd by being applied to the most current subjects and occurrences. The phrases and modes of combination in argument were caught by the most ignorant from the custom of the age, and their ridiculous misapplication of them is most amusingly exhibited in Costard; whilst examples suited only to the gravest propositions and impersonations, or apostrophes to abstract thoughts impersonated, which are in fact the natural language only of the most vehement agitations of the mind, are adopted by the coxcombry of Armado as mere artifices of ornament.

The same kind of intellectual action is exhibited in a more serious and elevated strain in many other parts of this play. Biron's speech at the end of the Fourth Act is an excellent specimen of it. It is logic clothed in rhetoric;—but observe how Shakespeare, in his two-fold being of poet and philosopher, avails himself of it to convey profound truths in the most lively images,—the whole remaining faithful to the character supposed to utter the lines, and the expressions themselves constituting a further development of that character:—

"Other slow arts entirely keep the brain:
And therefore finding barren practisers,
Scarce show a harvest of their heavy toil:
But love, first learned in a lady's eyes,
Lives not alone immured in the brain;
But, with the motion of all elements,
Courses as swift as thought in every power;
And gives to every power a double power,
Above their functions and their offices.
It adds a precious seeing to the eye,
A lover's eyes will gaze an eagle blind;
A lover's ear will hear the lowest sound,
When the suspicious head of theft is stopp'd:
Love's feeling is more soft and sensible,
Than are the tender horns of cockled snails;
Love's tongue proves dainty Bacchus gross in taste;
For valour, is not love a Hercules,
Still climbing trees in the Hesperides?
Subtle as Sphinx; as sweet and musical,
As bright Apollo's lute, strung with his hair;
And when love speaks, the voice of all the gods
Makes heaven drowsy with the harmony.
Never durst poet touch a pen to write,
Until his ink were tempered with love's sighs;
Oh, then his lines would ravish savage ears,
And plant in tyrants mild humility.

From women's eyes this doctrine I derive:
They sparkle still the right Promethean fire;
They are the books, the arts, the academes,
That show, contain, and nourish all the world;
Else, none at all in aught proves excellent;
Then fools you were these women to forswear;
Or, keeping what is sworn, you will prove fools.
For wisdom's sake, a word that all men love;
Or for love's sake, a word that loves all men;
Or for men's sake, the authors of these women;
Or women's sake, by whom we men are men;
Let us once lose our oaths, to find ourselves,
Or else we lose ourselves to keep our oaths:
It is religion to be thus forsworn:
For charity itself fulfils the law:
And who can sever love from charity?"—

This is quite a study;—sometimes you see this youthful god of poetry connecting disparate thoughts purely by means of resemblances in the words expressing them,—a thing in character in lighter comedy, especially of that kind in which Shakespeare delights, namely, the purposed display of wit, though sometimes too, disfiguring his graver scenes;—but more often you may see him doubling the natural connection or order of logical consequence in the thoughts by the introduction of an artificial and sought for resemblance in the words, as, for instance, in the third line of the play,—

"And then grace us in the disgrace of death;"—
this being a figure often having its force and propriety, as justified by the law of passion, which, inducing in the mind an unusual activity, seeks for means to waste its superfluity,—when in the highest degree—in lyric repetitions and sublime tautology—"At her feet he bowed, he fell, he lay down; at her feet he bowed, he fell; where he bowed, there he fell down dead,"—and, in lower degrees, in making the words themselves the subjects and materials of that surplus action, and for the same cause that agitates our limbs, and forces our very gestures into a tempest in states of high excitement.

The mere style of narration in Love's Labour's Lost, like that of Ægeon in the first scene of the Comedy of Errors, and of the Captain in the second scene of Macbeth, seems imitated with its defects and its beauties from Sir Philip Sidney; whose Arcadia, though not then published, was already well known in manuscript copies, and could hardly have escaped the notice and admiration of Shakespeare as the friend and client of the Earl of Southampton. The chief defect consists in the parentheses and parenthetic thoughts and descriptions, suited neither to the passion of the speaker, nor the purpose of the person to whom the information is to be given, but manifestly betraying the author himself,—not by way of continuous undersong, but—palpably, and so as to show themselves addressed to the general reader. However, it is not unimportant to notice how strong a presumption the diction and allusions of this play afford, that, though Shakespeare's acquirements in the dead languages might not be such as we suppose in a learned education, his habits had, nevertheless, been scholastic, and those of a student. For a young author's first work almost always bespeaks his recent pursuits, and his first observations of life are either drawn from the immediate employments of his youth, and from the characters and images most deeply impressed on his mind in the situations in which those employments had placed him;—or else they are fixed on such objects and occurrences in the world, as are easily connected with, and seem to bear upon, his studies and the hitherto exclusive subjects of his meditation. Just as Ben Jonson, who applied himself to the drama after having served in

Flanders, fills his earliest plays with true or pretended soldiers, the wrongs and neglects of the former, and the absurd boasts and knavery of their counterfeits. So Lessing's first comedies are placed in the universities, and consist of events and characters conceivable in an academic life.

I will only further remark the sweet and tempered gravity, with which Shakespeare in the end draws the only fitting moral which such a drama afforded. Here Rosaline rises up to the full height of Beatrice:—

"Ros. Oft have I heard of you, my lord Biron,
Before I saw you: and the world's large tongue
Proclaims you for a man replete with mocks;
Full of comparisons, and wounding flouts,
Which you on all estates will execute
That lie within the mercy of your wit:
To weed this wormwood from your fruitful brain,
And therewithal, to win me, if you please
(Without the which I am not to be won),
You shall this twelvemonth term from day to day
Visit the speechless sick, and still converse
With groaning wretches; and your talk shall be,
With all the fierce endeavour of your wit,
To enforce the pained impotent to smile.
Biron. To move wild laughter in the throat of death?
It cannot be; it is impossible;
Mirth cannot move a soul in agony.
Ros. Why, that's the way to choke a gibing spirit,
Whose influence is begot of that loose grace,
Which shallow laughing hearers give to fools;
A jest's prosperity lies in the ear
Of him that hears it, never in the tongue
Of him that makes it: then, if sickly ears,
Deaf'd with the clamours of their own dear groans,
Will hear your idle scorns, continue then,
And I will have you, and that fault withal:
But, if they will not, throw away that spirit,
And I shall find you empty of that fault,
Right joyful of your reformation."
Act v. sc. 2. In Biron's speech to the Princess:—

"And, therefore, like the eye,
Full of straying shapes, of habits, and of forms"—
either read stray, which I prefer; or throw full back to the preceding lines,—

"Like the eye, full
Of straying shapes," &c,
In the same scene:—

"Biron. And what to me, my love? and what to me?
Ros. You must be purged too, your sins are rank;
You are attaint with fault and perjury:
Therefore, if you my favour mean to get,

A twelvemonth shall you spend, and never rest,
But seek the weary beds of people sick."
There can be no doubt, indeed, about the propriety of expunging this speech of Rosaline's; it soils the very page that retains it. But I do not agree with Warburton and others in striking out the preceding line also. It is quite in Biron's character; and Rosaline, not answering it immediately, Dumain takes up the question for him, and, after he and Longaville are answered, Biron, with evident propriety, says:—

"Studies my mistress?" &c.
"Midsummer Night's Dream."

Act i. sc. 1.—

"Her. O cross! too high to be enthrall'd to low—
Lys. Or else misgrafted in respect of years;
Her. O spite! too old to be engaged to young—
Lys. Or else it stood upon the choice of friends;
Her. O hell! to chuse love by another's eye!"
There is no authority for any alteration;—but I never can help feeling how great an improvement it would be, if the two former of Hermia's exclamations were omitted;—the third and only appropriate one would then become a beauty, and most natural.

Ib. Helena's speech:—

"I will go tell him of fair Hermia's flight," &c.
I am convinced that Shakespeare availed himself of the title of this play in his own mind, and worked upon it as a dream throughout, but especially, and perhaps unpleasingly, in this broad determination of ungrateful treachery in Helena, so undisguisedly avowed to herself, and this, too, after the witty cool philosophising that precedes. The act itself is natural, and the resolve so to act is, I fear, likewise too true a picture of the lax hold which principles have on a woman's heart, when opposed to, or even separated from, passion and inclination. For women are less hypocrites to their own minds than men are, because in general they feel less proportionate abhorrence of moral evil in and for itself, and more of its outward consequences, as detection and loss of character, than men,—their natures being almost wholly extroitive. Still, however just in itself, the representation of this is not poetical; we shrink from it, and cannot harmonise it with the ideal.

Act ii. sc. 1. Theobald's edition—

"Through bush, through briar—
Through flood, through fire—"
What a noble pair of ears this worthy Theobald must have had! The eight amphimacers or cretics,—

"Ŏvĕr hĭll, ōvĕr dāle,
Thōrŏ' būsh, thōrŏ' brīar,
Ŏvĕr pārk, ōvĕr pāle,
Thrōrŏ' flōōd, thōrŏ' fīre"—
have a delightful effect on the ear in their sweet transition to the trochaic,—

"I dŏ wāndĕr ēv'ry whērĕ

Swīftĕr thăn thĕ mōōnĕs sphēre͝," &c.
The last words, as sustaining the rhyme, must be considered, as in fact they are, trochees in time.

It may be worth while to give some correct examples in English of the principle metrical feet:—

Pyrrhic or Dibrach, u u = bŏdy, spīrĭt.
Tribrach, u u u = nŏbŏdy, hastily pronounced.
Iambus, u - = dĕlīght.
Trochee, - u = līghtlȳ.
Spondee, - - = Gōd spāke.
The paucity of spondees in single words in English, and indeed in the modern languages in general, makes perhaps the greatest distinction, metrically considered, between them and the Greek and Latin.

Dactyl, - u u = mērrĭlȳ.
Anapæst, u u - = ă prŏpōs, or the first three syllables of cĕrĕmōny.
Amphibrachys, u - u = dĕlīghtfŭl.
Amphimacer, - u - = ōvĕr hīll.
Antibacchius, u - - = thĕ Lōrd Gōd.
Bacchius, - - u = Hēlvēllȳn.
Molossus, - - - = Jōhn Jāmes Jōnes.
These simple feet may suffice for understanding the metres of Shakespeare, for the greater part at least;—but Milton cannot be made harmoniously intelligible without the composite feet, the Ionics, Pæons, and Epitrites.

Ib. sc. 2. Titania's speech (Theobald, adopting Warburton's reading):—

"Which she, with pretty and with swimming gate
Follying (her womb then rich with my young squire)
Would imitate," &c.
Oh! oh! Heaven have mercy on poor Shakespeare, and also on Mr. Warburton's mind's eye!

Act v. sc. 1. Theseus' speech (Theobald):—

"And what poor [willing] duty cannot do,
Noble respect takes it in might, not merit."
To my ears it would read far more Shakespearian thus:—

"And what poor duty cannot do, yet would,
Noble respect," &c.
Ib. sc. 2.—

"Puck. Now the hungry lion roars,
And the wolf behowls the moon;
Whilst the heavy ploughman snores
All with weary task foredone," &c.
Very Anacreon in perfectness, proportion, grace, and spontaneity! So far it is Greek;—but then add, O! what wealth, what wild ranging, and yet what compression and condensation

of, English fancy! In truth, there is nothing in Anacreon more perfect than these thirty lines, or half so rich and imaginative. They form a speckless diamond.

"Comedy Of Errors."

The myriad-minded man, our, and all men's Shakespeare, has in this piece presented us with a legitimate farce in exactest consonance with the philosophical principles and character of farce, as distinguished from comedy and from entertainments. A proper farce is mainly distinguished from comedy by the licence allowed, and even required, in the fable, in order to produce strange and laughable situations. The story need not be probable, it is enough that it is possible. A comedy would scarcely allow even the two Antipholuses; because, although there have been instances of almost indistinguishable likeness in two persons, yet these are mere individual accidents, casus ludentis naturæ, and the verum will not excuse the inverisimile. But farce dares add the two Dromios, and is justified in so doing by the laws of its end and constitution. In a word, farces commence in a postulate, which must be granted.

"As You Like It."

Act i. sc. 1.

"Oli. What, boy!
Orla. Come, come, elder brother, you are too young in this.
Oli. Wilt thou lay hands on me, villain?"
There is a beauty here. The word "boy" naturally provokes and awakens in Orlando the sense of his manly powers; and with the retort of "elder brother," he grasps him with firm hands, and makes him feel he is no boy.

Ib.—

"Oli. Farewell, good Charles. Now will I stir this gamester: I hope, I shall see an end of him; for my soul, yet I know not why, hates nothing more than him. Yet he's gentle; never school'd, and yet learn'd; full of noble device; of all sorts enchantingly beloved! and, indeed, so much in the heart of the world, and especially of my own people, who best know him, that I am altogether misprised: but it shall not be so long; this wrestler shall clear all."

This has always appeared to me one of the most un-Shakespearian speeches in all the genuine works of our poet; yet I should be nothing surprised, and greatly pleased, to find it hereafter a fresh beauty, as has so often happened to me with other supposed defects of great men.—1810.

It is too venturous to charge a passage in Shakespeare with want of truth to nature; and yet at first sight this speech of Oliver's expresses truths, which it seems almost impossible that any mind should so distinctly, so livelily, and so voluntarily, have presented to itself, in connection with feelings and intentions so malignant, and so contrary to those which the qualities expressed would naturally have called forth. But I dare not say that this seeming unnaturalness is not in the nature of an abused wilfulness, when united with a strong intellect. In such characters there is sometimes a gloomy self-gratification in making the absoluteness of the will (sit pro ratione voluntas!) evident to themselves by setting the reason and the conscience in full array against it.—1818.

Ib. sc. 2.—

"Celia. If your saw yourself with your eyes, or knew yourself with your judgment, the fear of your adventure would counsel you to a more equal enterprise."

Surely it should be "our eyes" and "our judgment."

Ib. sc 3.—

"Cel. But is all this for your father?
Ros. No; some of it is for my child's father."
Theobald restores this as the reading of the older editions. It may be so: but who can doubt that it is a mistake for "my father's child," meaning herself? According to Theobald's note, a most indelicate anticipation is put into the mouth of Rosalind without reason;—and besides, what a strange thought, and how out of place and unintelligible!

Act iv. sc. 2.—

"Take thou no scorn
To wear the horn, the lusty horn;
It was a crest ere thou wast born."
I question whether there exists a parallel instance of a phrase, that like this of "horns" is universal in all languages, and yet for which no one has discovered even a plausible origin.

"Twelfth Night."

Act i. sc. 1. Duke's speech:—

... "So full of shapes is fancy,
That it alone is high fantastical."
Warburton's alteration of is into in is needless. "Fancy" may very well be interpreted "exclusive affection," or "passionate preference." Thus, bird-fanciers; gentlemen of the fancy, that is, amateurs of boxing, &c. The play of assimilation,—the meaning one sense chiefly, and yet keeping both senses in view, is perfectly Shakespearian.

Act ii. sc. 3. Sir Andrew's speech:—

An explanatory note on Pigrogromitus would have been more acceptable than Theobald's grand discovery that "lemon" ought to be "leman."

Ib. Sir Toby's speech (Warburton's note on the Peripatetic philosophy):—

"Shall we rouse the night-owl in a catch, that will draw three
"souls out of one weaver?"
O genuine, and inimitable (at least I hope so) Warburton! This note of thine, if but one in five millions, would be half a one too much.

Ib. sc. 4.—

"Duke. My life upon't, young though thou art, thine eye
Hath stay'd upon some favour that it loves;

Hath it not, boy?
Vio. A little, by your favour.
Duke. What kind of woman is't?"
And yet Viola was to have been presented to Orsino as a eunuch!—Act i. sc. 2. Viola's speech. Either she forgot this, or else she had altered her plan.

Ib.—

"Vio. A blank, my lord: she never told her love!—
But let concealment," &c.
After the first line (of which the last five words should be spoken with, and drop down in, a deep sigh), the actress ought to make a pause; and then start afresh, from the activity of thought, born of suppressed feelings, and which thought had accumulated during the brief interval, as vital heat under the skin during a dip in cold water.

Ib. sc. 5.—

"Fabian. Though our silence be drawn from us by cars, yet
peace."
Perhaps, "cables."

Act iii. sc. 1.—

"Clown. A sentence is but a cheveril glove to a good wit."
(Theobald's note.)
Theobald's etymology of "cheveril" is, of course, quite right;—but he is mistaken in supposing that there were no such things as gloves of chicken-skin. They were at one time a main article in chirocosmetics.

Act v. sc. 1. Clown's speech:—

"So that, conclusions to be as kisses, if your four negatives make
your two affirmatives, why, then, the worse for my friends, and the
better for my foes."
(Warburton reads "conclusion to be asked, is.")

Surely Warburton could never have wooed by kisses and won, or he would not have flounder-flatted so just and humorous, nor less pleasing than humorous, an image into so profound a nihility. In the name of love and wonder, do not four kisses make a double affirmative? The humour lies in the whispered "No!" and the inviting "Don't!" with which the maiden's kisses are accompanied, and thence compared to negatives, which by repetition constitute an affirmative.

"All's Well That Ends Well."

Act i. sc. 1.—

"Count. If the living be enemy to the grief, the excess makes
it soon mortal.
Bert. Madam, I desire your holy wishes.

Laf. How understand we that?"
Bertram and Lafeu, I imagine, both speak together,—Lafeu referring to the Countess's rather obscure remark.

Act ii. sc. 1. (Warburton's note.)

"King. ... let higher Italy
(Those 'bated, that inherit but the fall
Of the last monarchy) see, that you come
Not to woo honour, but to wed it."

It would be, I own, an audacious and unjustifiable change of the text; but yet, as a mere conjecture, I venture to suggest "bastards," for "'bated." As it stands, in spite of Warburton's note, I can make little or nothing of it. Why should the king except the then most illustrious states, which, as being republics, were the more truly inheritors of the Roman grandeur?—With my conjecture, the sense would be;—"let higher, or the more northern part of Italy—(unless 'higher' be a corruption for 'hir'd,'—the metre seeming to demand a monosyllable) (those bastards that inherit the infamy only of their fathers) see," &c. The following "woo" and "wed" are so far confirmative as they indicate Shakespeare's manner of connection by unmarked influences of association from some preceding metaphor. This it is which makes his style so peculiarly vital and organic. Likewise "those girls of Italy" strengthen the guess. The absurdity of Warburton's gloss, which represents the king calling Italy superior, and then excepting the only part the lords were going to visit, must strike every one.

Ib. sc. 3.—

"Laf. They say, miracles are past; and we have our philosophical
persons to make modern and familiar, things supernatural
and causeless."

Shakespeare, inspired, as it might seem, with all knowledge, here uses the word "causeless" in its strict philosophical sense;—cause being truly predicable only of phenomena, that is, things natural, and not of noumena, or things supernatural.

Act iii. sc. 5.—

"Dia. The Count Rousillon:—know you such a one?
Hel. But by the ear that hears most nobly of him;
His face I know not."

Shall we say here, that Shakespeare has unnecessarily made his loveliest character utter a lie?—Or shall we dare think that, where to deceive was necessary, he thought a pretended verbal verity a double crime, equally with the other a lie to the hearer, and at the same time an attempt to lie to one's own conscience?

"Merry Wives Of Windsor."

Act i. sc. 1.—

"Shal. The luce is the fresh fish, the salt fish is an old coat."
I cannot understand this. Perhaps there is a corruption both of words and speakers. Shallow no sooner corrects one mistake of Sir Hugh's, namely, "louse" for "luce," a pike, but the honest Welchman falls into another, namely, "cod" (baccalà). Cambrice—"cot" for coat.

"Shal. The luce is the fresh fish—
Evans. The salt fish is an old cot."
"Luce is a fresh fish, and not a louse;" says Shallow. "Aye, aye," quoth Sir Hugh; "the fresh fish is the luce; it is an old cod that is the salt fish." At all events, as the text stands, there is no sense at all in the words.

Ib. sc. 3—

"Fal. Now, the report goes, she has all the rule of her husband's
purse; He hath a legion of angels.
Pist. As many devils entertain; and To her, boy, say I."
Perhaps it is—

"As many devils enter (or enter'd) swine; and to her, boy,
say I:"—
a somewhat profane, but not un-Shakespearian, allusion to the "legion" in St. Luke's "gospel."

"Measure For Measure."

This play, which is Shakespeare's throughout, is to me the most painful—say rather, the only painful—part of his genuine works. The comic and tragic parts equally border on the μισητὸν,—the one being disgusting, the other horrible; and the pardon and marriage of Angelo not merely baffles the strong indignant claim of justice—(for cruelty, with lust and damnable baseness, cannot be forgiven, because we cannot conceive them as being morally repented of); but it is likewise degrading to the character of woman. Beaumont and Fletcher, who can follow Shakespeare in his errors only, have presented a still worse, because more loathsome and contradictory, instance of the same kind in the Night-Walker, in the marriage of Alathe to Algripe. Of the counter-balancing beauties of Measure for Measure, I need say nothing; for I have already remarked that the play is Shakespeare's throughout.

Act iii. sc. 1.—

"Ay, but to die, and go we know not where," &c.
"This natural fear of Claudio, from the antipathy we have to death, seems very little varied from that infamous wish of Mæcenas, recorded in the 101st epistle of Seneca:—

"Debilem facito manu,
Debilem pede, coxa" &c.—Warburton's note.
I cannot but think this rather a heroic resolve, than an infamous wish. It appears to me to be the grandest symptom of an immortal spirit, when even that bedimmed and overwhelmed spirit recked not of its own immortality, still to seek to be,—to be a mind, a will.

As fame is to reputation, so heaven is to an estate, or immediate advantage. The difference is, that the self-love of the former cannot exist but by a complete suppression and habitual supplantation of immediate selfishness. In one point of view, the miser is more estimable than the spendthrift;—only that the miser's present feelings are as much of the present as the spendthrift's. But cæteris paribus, that is, upon the supposition that whatever is good or lovely in the one coexists equally in the other, then, doubtless, the master of the present is less a selfish being, an animal, than he who lives for the moment with no inheritance in the future. Whatever can degrade man, is supposed in the latter case; whatever can elevate him, in the former. And as to self;—strange and generous self! that can only be such a self by a complete divestment of all that men call self,—of all that can make it either practically to others, or consciously to the individual himself, different from the human race in its ideal. Such self is but a perpetual religion, an inalienable acknowledgment of God, the sole basis and ground of being. In this sense, how can I love God, and not love myself, as far as it is of God?

Ib. sc. 2.—

"Pattern in himself to know,
Grace to stand, and virtue go."
Worse metre, indeed, but better English would be,—

"Grace to stand, virtue to go."

"Cymbeline."

Act i. sc. 1.—

"You do not meet a man, but frowns: our bloods
No more obey the heavens, than our courtiers'
Still seem, as does the king's."
There can be little doubt of Mr. Tyrwhitt's emendations of "courtiers" and "king," as to the sense;—only it is not impossible that Shakespeare's dramatic language may allow of the word "brows" or "faces" being understood after the word "courtiers'," which might then remain in the genitive case plural. But the nominative plural makes excellent sense, and is sufficiently elegant, and sounds to my ear Shakespearian. What, however, is meant by "our bloods no more obey the heavens?"—Dr. Johnson's assertion that "bloods" signify "countenances," is, I think, mistaken both in the thought conveyed—(for it was never a popular belief that the stars governed men's countenances)—and in the usage, which requires an antithesis of the blood,—or the temperament of the four humours, choler, melancholy, phlegm, and the red globules, or the sanguine portion, which was supposed not to be in our own power, but to be dependent on the influences of the heavenly bodies,—and the countenances which are in our power really, though from flattery we bring them into a no less apparent dependence on the sovereign, than the former are in actual dependence on the constellations.

I have sometimes thought that the word "courtiers" was a misprint for "countenances," arising from an anticipation, by foreglance of the compositor's eye, of the word "courtier" a few lines below. The written r is easily and often confounded with, the written n. The compositor read the first syllable court, and—his eye at the same time catching the word "courtier" lower down—he completed the word without reconsulting the copy. It is not unlikely that Shakespeare intended first to express, generally, the same thought, which a little afterwards he repeats with a particular application to the persons meant;—a common usage of the pronominal "our," where the speaker does not really mean to include himself; and the word "you" is an additional confirmation of the "our," being used in this place for "men" generally and indefinitely,—just as "you do not meet" is the same as "one does not meet."

Act i. sc. 1 Imogen's speech:—

... "My dearest husband,
I something fear my father's wrath; but nothing
(Always reserved my holy duty) what
His rage can do on me;"
Place the emphasis on "me"; for "rage" is a mere repetition of "wrath."

"Cym. O disloyal thing;
That should'st repair my youth; thou heapest
A year's age on me!"
How is it that the commentators take no notice of the un-Shakespearian defect in the metre of the second line, and what in Shakespeare is the same, in the harmony with the sense and feeling? Some word or words must have slipped out after "youth,"—possibly "and see":—

"That should'st repair my youth!—and see, thou heap'st," &c.
Ib. sc. 3. Pisanio's speech:—

... "For so long
As he could make me with this eye or ear
Distinguish him from others," &c.
But "this eye," in spite of the supposition of its being used δεικτικῶς, is very awkward. I should think that either "or" or "the" was Shakespeare's word;—

"As he could make me or with eye or ear."
Ib. sc. 6. Iachimo's speech:—

... "Hath nature given them eyes
To see this vaulted arch, and the rich crop
Of sea and land, which can distinguish 'twixt
The fiery orbs above, and the twinn'd stones
Upon the number'd beach."
I would suggest "cope" for "crop." As to "twinn'd stones"—may it not be a bold catachresis for muscles, cockles, and other empty shells with hinges, which are truly twinned? I would take Dr. Farmer's "umber'd," which I had proposed before I ever heard of its having been already offered by him: but I do not adopt his interpretation of the word, which I think is not derived from umbra, a shade, but from umber, a dingy yellow-brown soil, which most commonly forms the mass of the sludge on the sea-shore, and on the banks of tide-rivers at low water. One other possible interpretation of this sentence has occurred to me, just barely worth mentioning;—that the "twinn'd stones" are the augrim stones upon the number'd beech,—that is, the astronomical tables of beech-wood.

Act v. sc. 5.—

"Sooth. When, as a lion's whelp," &c.
It is not easy to conjecture why Shakespeare should have introduced this ludicrous scroll, which answers no one purpose, either propulsive, or explicatory, unless as a joke on etymology.

"Titus Andronicus."

Act i. sc. 1. Theobald's note:—

"I never heard it so much as intimated, that he (Shakespeare) had turned his genius to stage-writing, before he associated with the players, and became one of their body."
That Shakespeare never "turned his genius to stage-writing," as Theobald most Theobaldice phrases it, before he became an actor, is an assertion of about as much authority as the precious story that he left Stratford for deer-stealing, and that he lived by holding gentlemen's horses at the doors of the theatre, and other trash of that arch-gossip, old Aubrey. The metre is an argument against Titus Andronicus being Shakespeare's, worth a score such chronological surmises. Yet I incline to think that both in this play and in Jeronymo, Shakespeare wrote some passages, and that they are the earliest of his compositions.

Act v. sc. 2. I think it not improbable that the lines from—

"I am not mad; I know thee well enough;
to

So thou destroy Rapine, and Murder there"—
were written by Shakespeare in his earliest period. But instead of the text—

"Revenge, which makes the foul offenders quake.
Tit. Art thou Revenge? and art thou sent to me?"—
the words in italics ought to be omitted.

"Troilus And Cressida."

"Mr. Pope (after Dryden) informs us that the story of Troilus and Cressida was originally the work of one Lollius, a Lombard: but Dryden goes yet further; he declares it to have been written in Latin verse, and that Chaucer translated it. Lollius was a historiographer of Urbino in Italy."—Note in Stockdale's edition, 1807.
"Lollius was a historiographer of Urbino in Italy." So affirms the notary to whom the Sieur Stockdale committed the disfaciménto of Ayscough's excellent edition of Shakespeare. Pity that the researchful notary has not either told us in what century, and of what history, he was a writer, or been simply content to depose, that Lollius, if a writer of that name existed at all, was a somewhat somewhere. The notary speaks of the Troy Boke of Lydgate, printed in 1513. I have never seen it; but I deeply regret that Chalmers did not substitute the whole of Lydgate's works from the MSS. extant, for the almost worthless Gower.

The Troilus and Cressida of Shakespeare can scarcely be classed with his dramas of Greek and Roman history; but it forms an intermediate link between the fictitious Greek and Roman histories, which we may call legendary dramas, and the proper ancient histories,—that is, between the Pericles or Titus Andronicus, and the Coriolanus or Julius Cæsar. Cymbeline is a congener with Pericles, and distinguished from Lear by not having any declared prominent object. But where shall we class the Timon of Athens? Perhaps immediately below Lear. It is a Lear of the satirical drama; a Lear of domestic or ordinary life;—a local eddy of passion on the high road of society, while all around is the week-day goings on of wind and weather; a Lear, therefore, without its soul-searching flashes, its ear-cleaving thunder-claps, its meteoric splendours,—without the contagion and the fearful sympathies of nature, the fates, the furies, the frenzied elements, dancing in and out, now breaking through and scattering,—now hand in hand with,—the fierce or fantastic group of human passions, crimes, and anguishes, reeling on the unsteady ground, in a wild harmony to the shock and the swell of an earthquake. But my present subject was Troilus and Cressida; and I suppose that, scarcely knowing what to say of it, I by a cunning of instinct ran off to subjects on which I should find it difficult not to say too much, though certain after all that I should still leave the better part unsaid, and the gleaning for others richer than my own harvest.

Indeed, there is no one of Shakespeare's plays harder to characterise. The name and the remembrances connected with it, prepare us for the representation of attachment no less faithful than fervent on the side of the youth, and of sudden and shameless inconstancy on the part of the lady. And this is, indeed, as the gold thread on which the scenes are strung, though often kept out of sight and out of mind by gems of greater value than itself. But as Shakespeare calls forth nothing from the mausoleum of history, or the catacombs of tradition, without giving, or eliciting, some permanent and general interest, and brings forward no subject which he does not moralise or intellectualise,—so here he has drawn in Cressida the portrait of a vehement passion, that, having its true origin and proper cause in warmth of temperament, fastens on, rather than fixes to, some one object by liking and temporary preference.

"There's language in her eye, her cheek, her lip,
Nay, her foot speaks; her wanton spirit looks out
At every joint and motive of her body."
This Shakespeare has contrasted with the profound affection represented in Troilus, and alone worthy the name of love;—affection, passionate indeed,—swoln with the confluence of youthful instincts and youthful fancy, and growing in the radiance of hope newly risen, in short, enlarged by the collective sympathies of nature;—but still having a depth of calmer element in a will stronger than desire, more entire than choice, and which gives permanence to its own act by converting it into faith and duty. Hence, with excellent judgment, and with an excellence higher than mere judgment can give, at the close of the play, when Cressida has sunk into infamy below retrieval and beneath hope, the same will, which had been the substance and the basis of his love, while the restless pleasures and passionate longings, like sea-waves, had tossed but on its surface,—this same moral energy is represented as snatching him aloof from all neighbourhood with her dishonour, from all lingering fondness and languishing regrets, whilst it rushes with him into other and nobler duties, and deepens the channel, which his heroic brother's death had left empty for its collected flood. Yet another secondary and subordinate purpose Shakespeare has inwoven with his delineation of these two characters,—that of opposing the inferior civilisation, but purer morals, of the Trojans to the refinements, deep policy, but duplicity and sensual corruptions of the Greeks.

To all this, however, so little comparative projection is given,—nay, the masterly group of Agamemnon, Nestor, and Ulysses, and, still more in advance, that of Achilles, Ajax, and Thersites, so manifestly occupying the fore-ground, that the subservience and vassalage of strength and animal courage to intellect and policy seems to be the lesson most often in our poet's view, and which he has taken little pains to connect with the former more interesting moral impersonated in the titular hero and heroine of the drama. But I am half inclined to believe, that Shakespeare's main object, or shall I rather say his ruling impulse, was to translate the poetic heroes of paganism into the not less rude, but more intellectually vigorous, and more featurely, warriors of Christian chivalry,—and to substantiate the distinct and graceful profiles or outlines of the Homeric epic into the flesh and blood of the romantic drama;—in short, to give a grand history-piece in the robust style of Albert Durer.

The character of Thersites, in particular, well deserves a more careful examination, as the Caliban of demagogic life;—the admirable portrait of intellectual power deserted by all grace, all moral principle, all not momentary impulse;—just wise enough to detect the weak head, and fool enough to provoke the armed fist of his betters;—one whom malcontent Achilles can inveigle from malcontent Ajax, under the one condition, that he shall be called on to do nothing but abuse and slander, and that he shall be allowed to abuse as much and as purulently as he likes, that is, as he can;—in short, a mule,—quarrelsome by the original discord of his nature;—a slave by tenure of his own baseness,—made to bray and be brayed at, to despise and be despicable. "Aye, Sir, but say what you will, he is a very clever fellow, though the best friends will fall out. There was a time when Ajax thought he deserved to have a statue of gold erected to him and handsome Achilles, at the head of the Myrmidons, gave no little credit to his friend Thersites!"

Act iv. sc. 5. Speech of Ulysses:—

"O, these encounterers, so glib of tongue,
That give a coasting welcome ere it comes"—
Should it be "accosting?" "Accost her, knight, accost!" in the Twelfth Night. Yet there sounds a something so Shakespearian in the phrase—"give a coasting welcome" ("coasting" being taken as the epithet and adjective of "welcome"), that had the following words been, "ere they land," instead of "ere it comes," I should have preferred the interpretation. The sense now is, "that give welcome to a salute ere it comes."

"Coriolanus."

This play illustrates the wonderfully philosophic impartiality of Shakespeare's politics. His own country's history furnished him with no matter but what was too recent to be devoted to patriotism. Besides, he knew that the instruction of ancient history would seem more dispassionate. In Coriolanus and Julius Cæsar, you see Shakespeare's good-natured laugh at mobs. Compare this with Sir Thomas Brown's aristocracy of spirit.

Act i. sc. 1. Marcius' speech:—

... "He that depends
Upon your favours, swims with fins of lead,
And hews down oaks with rushes. Hang ye! Trust ye?"
I suspect that Shakespeare wrote it transposed!

"Trust ye? Hang ye!"
Ib. sc. 10. Speech of Aufidius:—

... "Mine emulation
Hath not that honour in't, it had; for where
I thought to crush him in an equal force,
True sword to sword; I'll potch at him some way
Or wrath, or craft may get him.—
... My valour (poison'd
With only suffering stain by him) for him

Shall fly out of itself: nor sleep, nor sanctuary,
Being naked, sick, nor fane, nor capitol,
The prayers of priests, nor times of sacrifices,
Embankments all of fury, shall lift up
Their rotten privilege and custom 'gainst
My hate to Marcius."

I have such deep faith in Shakespeare's heart-lore, that I take for granted that this is in nature, and not as a mere anomaly; although I cannot in myself discover any germ of possible feeling, which could wax and unfold itself into such sentiment as this. However, I perceive that in this speech is meant to be contained a prevention of shock at the after-change in Aufidius's character.

Act ii. sc. 1. Speech of Menenius:—

"The most sovereign prescription in Galen," &c.
Was it without, or in contempt of, historical information that Shakespeare made the contemporaries of Coriolanus quote Cato and Galen? I cannot decide to my own satisfaction.

Ib. sc. 3. Speech of Coriolanus:—

"Why in this wolvish toge should I stand here"
That the gown of the candidate was of whitened wool, we know. Does "wolvish" or "woolvish" mean "made of wool?" If it means "wolfish," what is the sense?

Act iv. sc. 7. Speech of Aufidius:—

"All places yield to him ere he sits down," &c.
I have always thought this, in itself so beautiful speech, the least explicable from the mood and full intention of the speaker of any in the whole works of Shakespeare. I cherish the hope that I am mistaken, and that, becoming wiser, I shall discover some profound excellence in that, in which I now appear to detect an imperfection.

"Julius Cæsar."

Act i. sc. 1.—

"Mar. What meanest thou by that? Mend me, thou saucy
fellow!"
The speeches of Flavius and Marullus are in blank verse. Wherever regular metre can be rendered truly imitative of character, passion, or personal rank, Shakespeare seldom, if ever, neglects it. Hence this line should be read:—

"What mean'st by that? mend me, thou saucy fellow!"
I say regular metre: for even the prose has in the highest and lowest dramatic personage, a Cobbler or a Hamlet, a rhythm so felicitous and so severally appropriate, as to be a virtual metre.

Ib. sc. 2.—

"Bru. A soothsayer bids you beware the Ides of March."

If my ear does not deceive me, the metre of this line was meant to express that sort of mild philosophic contempt, characterising Brutus even in his first casual speech. The line is a trimeter,—each dipodia containing two accented and two unaccented syllables, but variously arranged, as thus:—

u - - u | - u u - | u - u -
A soothsayer | bids you beware | the Ides of March.
Ib. Speech of Brutus:—

"Set honour in one eye, and death i' the other,
And I will look on both indifferently."
Warburton would read "death" for "both;" but I prefer the old text. There are here three things, the public good, the individual Brutus' honour, and his death. The latter two so balanced each other, that he could decide for the first by equipoise; nay—the thought growing—that honour had more weight than death. That Cassius understood it as Warburton, is the beauty of Cassius as contrasted with Brutus.

Ib. Cæsar's speech:—

... "He loves no plays
As thou dost, Antony; he hears no music," &c.
"This is not a trivial observation, nor does our poet mean barely by it, that Cassius was not a merry, sprightly man; but that he had not a due temperament of harmony in his disposition."—Theobald's note.
O Theobald! what a commentator wast thou, when thou would'st affect to understand Shakespeare, instead of contenting thyself with collating the text! The meaning here is too deep for a line ten-fold the length of thine to fathom.

Ib. sc. 3. Cæsar's speech:—

"Be factious for redress of all these griefs;
And I will set this foot of mine as far,
As who goes farthest."
I understand it thus: "You have spoken as a conspirator; be so in fact, and I will join you. Act on your principles, and realize them in a fact."

Act ii. sc. 1. Speech of Brutus:—

"It must be by his death; and, for my part,
I know no personal cause to spurn at him,
But for the general. He would be crown'd:
How that might change his nature, there's the question.
... And, to speak truth of Cæsar,
I have not known when his affections sway'd
More than his reason.
... So Cæsar may;
Then, lest he may, prevent."
This speech is singular;—at least, I do not at present see into Shakespeare's motive, his rationale, or in what point of view he meant Brutus' character to appear. For surely—(this, I mean, is what I say to myself, with my present quantum of insight, only modified by my experience in how many instances I have ripened into a perception of beauties, where I had before descried faults;) surely, nothing can seem more discordant with our historical

preconceptions of Brutus, or more lowering to the intellect of the Stoico-Platonic tyrannicide, than the tenets here attributed to him—to him, the stern Roman republican; namely,—that he would have no objection to a king, or to Cæsar, a monarch in Rome, would Cæsar but be as good a monarch as he now seems disposed to be! How, too, could Brutus say that he found no personal cause—none in Cæsar's past conduct as a man? Had he not passed the Rubicon? Had he not entered Rome as a conqueror? Had he not placed his Gauls in the Senate?—Shakespeare, it may be said, has not brought these things forward—True;—and this is just the ground of my perplexity. What character did Shakespeare mean his Brutus to be?

Ib. Speech of Brutus:—

"For if thou path, thy native semblance on."
Surely, there need be no scruple in treating this "path" as a mere misprint or mis-script for "put." In what place does Shakespeare—where does any other writer of the same age—use "path" as a verb for "walk?"

Ib. sc. 2. Cæsar's speech:—

"She dreamt to-night, she saw my statue."
No doubt, it should be statua, as in the same age, they more often pronounced "heroes" as a trisyllable than dissyllable. A modern tragic poet would have written,—

"Last night she dreamt that she my statue saw."
But Shakespeare never avails himself of the supposed license of transposition, merely for the metre. There is always some logic either of thought or passion to justify it.

Act iii. sc. 1. Antony's speech:—

"Pardon me, Julius—here wast thou bay'd, brave hart:
Here didst thou fall; and here thy hunters stand
Sign'd in thy spoil, and crimson'd in thy lethe.
O world! thou wast the forest to this hart,
And this, indeed, O world! the heart of thee."
I doubt the genuineness of the last two lines;—not because they are vile; but first, on account of the rhythm, which is not Shakespearian, but just the very tune of some old play, from which the actor might have interpolated them;—and secondly, because they interrupt, not only the sense and connection, but likewise the flow both of the passion, and (what is with me still more decisive) of the Shakespearian link of association. As with many another parenthesis or gloss slipt into the text, we have only to read the passage without it, to see that it never was in it. I venture to say there is no instance in Shakespeare fairly like this. Conceits he has; but they not only rise out of some word in the lines before, but also lead to the thought in the lines following. Here the conceit is a mere alien: Antony forgets an image, when he is even touching it, and then recollects it, when the thought last in his mind must have led him away from it.

Act iv. sc. 3. Speech of Brutus:—

... "What, shall one of us,
That struck the foremost man of all this world,
But for supporting robbers."

This seemingly strange assertion of Brutus is unhappily verified in the present day. What is an immense army, in which the lust of plunder has quenched all the duties of the citizen, other than a horde of robbers, or differenced only as fiends are from ordinarily reprobate men? Cæsar supported, and was supported by, such as these;—and even so Buonaparte in our days.

I know no part of Shakespeare that more impresses on me the belief of his genius being superhuman, than this scene between Brutus and Cassius. In the Gnostic heresy it might have been credited with less absurdity than most of their dogmas, that the Supreme had employed him to create, previously to his function of representing, characters.

"Antony And Cleopatra."

Shakespeare can be complimented only by comparison with himself: all other eulogies are either heterogeneous, as when they are in reference to Spenser or Milton; or they are flat truisms, as when he is gravely preferred to Corneille, Racine, or even his own immediate successors, Beaumont and Fletcher, Massinger and the rest. The highest praise, or rather form of praise, of this play, which I can offer in my own mind, is the doubt which the perusal always occasions in me, whether the Antony and Cleopatra is not, in all exhibitions of a giant power in its strength and vigour of maturity, a formidable rival of Macbeth, Lear, Hamlet, and Othello. Feliciter audax is the motto for its style comparatively with that of Shakespeare's other works, even as it is the general motto of all his works compared with those of other poets. Be it remembered, too, that this happy valiancy of style is but the representative and result of all the material excellencies so expressed.

This play should be perused in mental contrast with Romeo and Juliet;—as the love of passion and appetite opposed to the love of affection and instinct. But the art displayed in the character of Cleopatra is profound; in this, especially, that the sense of criminality in her passion is lessened by our insight into its depth and energy, at the very moment that we cannot but perceive that the passion itself springs out of the habitual craving of a licentious nature, and that it is supported and reinforced by voluntary stimulus and sought-for associations, instead of blossoming out of spontaneous emotion.

Of all Shakespeare's historical plays, Antony and Cleopatra is by far the most wonderful. There is not one in which he has followed history so minutely, and yet there are few in which he impresses the notion of angelic strength so much;—perhaps none in which he impresses it more strongly. This is greatly owing to the manner in which the fiery force is sustained throughout, and to the numerous momentary flashes of nature counteracting the historic abstraction. As a wonderful specimen of the way in which Shakespeare lives up to the very end of this play, read the last part of the concluding scene. And if you would feel the judgment as well as the genius of Shakespeare in your heart's core, compare this astonishing drama with Dryden's All For Love.

Act i. sc. 1. Philo's speech:—

... "His captain's heart
Which in the scuffles of great fights hath burst
The buckles on his breast, reneges all temper."
It should be "reneagues," or "reniegues," as "fatigues," &c.

Ib.—

"Take but good note, and you shall see in him
The triple pillar of the world transform'd
Into a strumpet's fool."

Warburton's conjecture of "stool" is ingenious, and would be a probable reading, if the scene opening had discovered Antony with Cleopatra on his lap. But, represented as he is walking and jesting with her, "fool" must be the word. Warburton's objection is shallow, and implies that he confounded the dramatic with the epic style. The "pillar" of a state is so common a metaphor as to have lost the image in the thing meant to be imaged.

Ib. sc. 2.—

... "Much is breeding;
Which, like the courser's hair, hath yet but life,
And not a serpent's poison."

This is so far true to appearance, that a horse-hair, "laid," as Hollinshed says, "in a pail of water," will become the supporter of seemingly one worm, though probably of an immense number of small slimy water-lice. The hair will twirl round a finger, and sensibly compress it. It is a common experiment with school boys in Cumberland and Westmoreland.

Act ii. sc. 2. Speech of Enobarbus:—

"Her gentlewomen, like the Nereides,
So many mermaids, tended her i' th' eyes,
And made their bends adornings. At the helm
A seeming mermaid steers."

I have the greatest difficulty in believing that Shakespeare wrote the first "mermaids." He never, I think, would have so weakened by useless anticipation the fine image immediately following. The epithet "seeming" becomes so extremely improper after the whole number had been positively called "so many mermaids."

"Timon Of Athens."

Act i. sc. 1.—

"Tim. The man is honest.
Old Ath. Therefore he will be, Timon.
His honesty rewards him in itself."

Warburton's comment—"If the man be honest, for that reason he will be so in this, and not endeavour at the injustice of gaining my daughter without my consent"—is, like almost all his comments, ingenious in blunder; he can never see any other writer's thoughts for the mist-working swarm of his own. The meaning of the first line the poet himself explains, or rather unfolds, in the second. "The man is honest!"—"True;—and for that very cause, and with no additional or extrinsic motive, he will be so. No man can be justly called honest, who is not so for honesty's sake, itself including its own reward." Note, that "honesty" in Shakespeare's age retained much of its old dignity, and that contradistinction of the honestum from the utile, in which its very essence and definition consist. If it be honestum, it cannot depend on the utile.

Ib. Speech of Apemantus, printed as prose in Theobald's edition:—

"So, so! aches contract, and starve your supple joints!"

I may remark here the fineness of Shakespeare's sense of musical period, which would almost by itself have suggested (if the hundred positive proofs had not been extant) that the word "aches" was then ad libitum, a dissyllable—aitches. For read it "aches," in this sentence, and I would challenge you to find any period in Shakespeare's writings with the same musical or, rather dissonant, notation. Try the one, and then the other, by your ear, reading the sentence aloud, first with the word as a dissyllable and then as a monosyllable, and you will feel what I mean.

Ib. sc. 2. Cupid's speech: Warburton's correction of—

"There taste, touch, all pleas'd from thy table rise"—
into

"Th' ear, taste, touch, smell," &c.
This is indeed an excellent emendation.

Act ii. sc. 1. Senator's speech:—

... "Nor then silenc'd with
"Commend me to your master"—and the cap
Plays in the right hand, thus."
Either, methinks, "plays" should be "play'd," or "and" should be changed to "while." I can certainly understand it as a parenthesis, an interadditive of scorn; but it does not sound to my ear as in Shakespeare's manner.

Ib. sc. 2. Timon's speech (Theobald):—

"And that unaptness made you minister,
Thus to excuse yourself."
Read your;—at least I cannot otherwise understand the line. You made my chance indisposition and occasional inaptness your minister—that is, the ground on which you now excuse yourself. Or, perhaps, no correction is necessary, if we construe "made you" as "did you make;" "and that unaptness did you make help you thus to excuse yourself." But the former seems more in Shakespeare's manner, and is less liable to be misunderstood.

Act iii. sc. 3. Servant's speech:—

"How fairly this lord strives to appear foul!—takes virtuous copies to be wicked; like those that under hot, ardent zeal would set whole realms on fire. Of such a nature is his politic love."
This latter clause I grievously suspect to have been an addition of the players, which had hit, and, being constantly applauded, procured a settled occupation in the prompter's copy. Not that Shakespeare does not elsewhere sneer at the Puritans; but here it is introduced so nolenter volenter (excuse the phrase) by the head and shoulders!—and is besides so much more likely to have been conceived in the age of Charles I.

Act iv. sc. 3. Timon's speech:—

"Raise me this beggar, and deny't that lord."
Warburton reads "denude."

I cannot see the necessity of this alteration. The editors and commentators are, all of them, ready enough to cry out against Shakespeare's laxities and licenses of style, forgetting that he is not merely a poet, but a dramatic poet; that, when the head and the heart are swelling with fulness, a man does not ask himself whether he has grammatically arranged, but only whether (the context taken in) he has conveyed his meaning. "Deny" is here clearly equal to "withhold;" and the "it," quite in the genius of vehement conversation, which a syntaxist explains by ellipses and subauditurs in a Greek or Latin classic, yet triumphs over as ignorances in a contemporary, refers to accidental and artificial rank or elevation, implied in the verb "raise." Besides, does the word "denude" occur in any writer before, or of, Shakespeare's age?

"Romeo And Juliet."

I have previously had occasion to speak at large on the subject of the three unities of time, place, and action, as applied to the drama in the abstract, and to the particular stage for which Shakespeare wrote, as far as he can be said to have written for any stage but that of the universal mind. I hope I have in some measure succeeded in demonstrating that the former two, instead of being rules, were mere inconveniences attached to the local peculiarities of the Athenian drama; that the last alone deserved the name of a principle, and that in the preservation of this unity Shakespeare stood pre-eminent. Yet, instead of unity of action, I should greatly prefer the more appropriate, though scholastic and uncouth, words homogeneity, proportionateness, and totality of interest,—expressions, which involve the distinction, or rather the essential difference, betwixt the shaping skill of mechanical talent, and the creative, productive, life-power of inspired genius. In the former each part is separately conceived, and then by a succeeding act put together;—not as watches are made for wholesale—(for there each part supposes a pre-conception of the whole in some mind),—but more like pictures on a motley screen. Whence arises the harmony that strikes us in the wildest natural landscapes,—in the relative shapes of rocks, the harmony of colours in the heaths, ferns, and lichens, the leaves of the beech and the oak, the stems and rich brown branches of the birch and other mountain trees, varying from verging autumn to returning spring,—compared with the visual effect from the greater number of artificial plantations?—From this, that the natural landscape is effected, as it were, by a single energy modified ab intra in each component part. And as this is the particular excellence of the Shakespearian drama generally, so is it especially characteristic of the Romeo and Juliet.

The groundwork of the tale is altogether in family life, and the events of the play have their first origin in family feuds. Filmy as are the eyes of party-spirit, at once dim and truculent, still there is commonly some real or supposed object in view, or principle to be maintained; and though but the twisted wires on the plate of rosin in the preparation for electrical pictures, it is still a guide in some degree, an assimilation to an outline. But in family quarrels, which have proved scarcely less injurious to states, wilfulness, and precipitancy, and passion from mere habit and custom can alone be expected. With his accustomed judgment, Shakespeare has begun by placing before us a lively picture of all the impulses of the play; and, as nature ever presents two sides, one for Heraclitus, and one for Democritus, he has, by way of prelude, shown the laughable absurdity of the evil by the contagion of it reaching the servants who have so little to do with it, but who are under the necessity of letting the superfluity of sensoreal power fly off through the escape-valve of wit-combats, and of quarrelling with weapons of sharper edge, all in humble imitation of their masters. Yet there is a sort of unhired fidelity, an ourishness about all this that makes it rest pleasant on one's feelings. All the first scene, down to the conclusion of the Prince's speech, is a motley dance of all ranks and ages to one tune, as if the horn of Huon had been playing behind the scenes.

Benvolio's speech:—

"Madam, an hour before the worshipp'd sun
Peer'd forth the golden window of the east"—
and, far more strikingly, the following speech of old Montague:—

"Many a morning hath he there been seen
With tears augmenting the fresh morning dew"—
prove that Shakespeare meant the Romeo and Juliet to approach to a poem, which, and indeed its early date, may be also inferred from the multitude of rhyming couplets throughout. And if we are right, from the internal evidence, in pronouncing this one of Shakespeare's early dramas, it affords a strong instance of the fineness of his insight into the nature of the passions, that Romeo is introduced already love-bewildered. The necessity of loving creates an object for itself in man and woman; and yet there is a difference in this respect between the sexes, though only to be known by a perception of it. It would have displeased us if Juliet had been represented as already in love, or as fancying herself so;— but no one, I believe, ever experiences any shock at Romeo's forgetting his Rosaline, who had been a mere name for the yearning of his youthful imagination, and rushing into his passion for Juliet. Rosaline was a mere creation of his fancy; and we should remark the boastful positiveness of Romeo in a love of his own making, which is never shown where love is really near the heart.

"When the devout religion of mine eye
Maintains such falsehood, then turn tears to fires!
One fairer than my love! the all-seeing sun
Ne'er saw her match, since first the world begun."
The character of the Nurse is the nearest of any thing in Shakespeare to a direct borrowing from mere observation; and the reason is, that as in infancy and childhood the individual in nature is a representative of a class,—just as in describing one larch tree, you generalise a grove of them,—so it is nearly as much so in old age. The generalisation is done to the poet's hand. Here you have the garrulity of age strengthened by the feelings of a long-trusted servant, whose sympathy with the mother's affections gives her privileges and rank in the household; and observe the mode of connection by accidents of time and place, and the childlike fondness of repetition in a second childhood, and also that happy humble, ducking under, yet constant resurgence against, the check of her superiors!—

"Yes, madam!—Yet I cannot choose but laugh," &c.
In the fourth scene we have Mercutio introduced to us. O! how shall I describe that exquisite ebullience and overflow of youthful life, wafted on over the laughing waves of pleasure and prosperity, as a wanton beauty that distorts the face on which she knows her lover is gazing enraptured, and wrinkles her forehead in the triumph of its smoothness! Wit ever wakeful, fancy busy and procreative as an insect, courage, an easy mind that, without cares of its own, is at once disposed to laugh away those of others, and yet to be interested in them,—these and all congenial qualities, melting into the common copula of them all, the man of rank and the gentleman, with all its excellencies and all its weaknesses, constitute the character of Mercutio!

Act i. sc. 5.—

"Tyb. It fits when such a villain is a guest;
I'll not endure him.
Cap. He shall be endur'd.
What, goodman boy!—I say, he shall:—Go to;—
Am I the master here, or you?—Go to.
You'll not endure him!—God shall mend my soul—
You'll make a mutiny among my guests!
You will set cock-a-hoop! you'll be the man!
Tyb. Why, uncle, 'tis a shame.
Cap. Go to, go to,
You are a saucy boy!" &c.

How admirable is the old man's impetuosity at once contrasting, yet harmonised, with young Tybalt's quarrelsome violence! But it would be endless to repeat observations of this sort. Every leaf is different on an oak tree; but still we can only say—our tongues defrauding our eyes— "This is another oak-leaf!"

Act ii. sc. 2. The garden scene.

Take notice in this enchanting scene of the contrast of Romeo's love with his former fancy; and weigh the skill shown in justifying him from his inconstancy by making us feel the difference of his passion. Yet this, too, is a love in, although not merely of, the imagination.

Ib.—

"Jul. Well, do not swear; although I joy in thee,
I have no joy in this contract to-night:
It is too rash, too unadvised, too sudden," &c.

With love, pure love, there is always an anxiety for the safety of the object, a disinterestedness, by which it is distinguished from the counterfeits of its name. Compare this scene with Act iii. sc. 1 of the Tempest. I do not know a more wonderful instance of Shakespeare's mastery in playing a distinctly rememberable variety on the same remembered air, than in the transporting love confessions of Romeo and Juliet and Ferdinand and Miranda. There seems more passion in the one, and more dignity in the other; yet you feel that the sweet girlish lingering and busy movement of Juliet, and the calmer and more maidenly fondness of Miranda, might easily pass into each other.

Ib. sc. 3. The Friar's speech.

The reverend character of the Friar, like all Shakespeare's representations of the great professions, is very delightful and tranquillising, yet it is no digression, but immediately necessary to the carrying on of the plot.

Ib. sc. 4.—

"Rom. Good morrow to you both. What counterfeit did I give you?" &c.
Compare again Romeo's half-exerted, and half real, ease of mind with his first manner when in love with Rosaline! His will had come to the clenching point.

Ib. sc. 6.—

"Rom. Do thou but close our hands with holy words,
Then love-devouring death do what he dare,

It is enough I may but call her mine."

The precipitancy, which is the character of the play, is well marked in this short scene of waiting for Juliet's arrival.

Act iii. sc. 1.—

"Mer. No, 'tis not so deep as a well, nor so wide as a church door; but 'tis enough: 'twill serve: ask for me to-morrow, and you shall find me a grave man," &c.

How fine an effect the wit and raillery habitual to Mercutio, even struggling with his pain, give to Romeo's following speech, and at the same time so completely justifying his passionate revenge on Tybalt!

Ib. Benvolio's speech:—

... "But that he tilts
With piercing steel at bold Mercutio's breast."
This small portion of untruth in Benvolio's narrative is finely conceived.

Ib. sc. 2. Juliet's speech:—

"For thou wilt lie upon the wings of night
Whiter than new snow on a raven's back."
Indeed the whole of this speech is imagination strained to the highest; and observe the blessed effect on the purity of the mind. What would Dryden have made of it?

Ib.—

"Nurse. Shame come to Romeo.
Jul. Blister'd be thy tongue
For such a wish!"
Note the Nurse's mistake of the mind's audible struggles with itself for its decision in toto.

Ib. sc. 3. Romeo's speech:—

"'Tis torture, and not mercy: heaven's here,
Where Juliet lives," &c.
All deep passions are a sort of atheists, that believe no future.

Ib. sc. 5.—

"Cap. Soft! take me with you, take me with you, wife—How!
will she none?" &c.
A noble scene! Don't I see it with my own eyes?—Yes! but not with Juliet's. And observe in Capulet's last speech in this scene his mistake, as if love's causes were capable of being generalised.

Act iv. sc. 3. Juliet's speech.:—

"O, look! methinks I see my cousin's ghost
Seeking out Romeo, that did spit his body
Upon a rapier's point:—Stay, Tybalt, stay!—

Romeo, I come! this do I drink to thee."

Shakespeare provides for the finest decencies. It would have been too bold a thing for a girl of fifteen;—but she swallows the draught in a fit of fright.

Ib. sc. 5.—

As the audience know that Juliet is not dead, this scene is, perhaps, excusable. But it is a strong warning to minor dramatists not to introduce at one time many separate characters agitated by one and the same circumstance. It is difficult to understand what effect, whether that of pity or of laughter, Shakespeare meant to produce;—the occasion and the characteristic speeches are so little in harmony! For example, what the Nurse says is excellently suited to the Nurse's character, but grotesquely unsuited to the occasion.

Act v. sc. 1. Romeo's speech:—

... "O mischief! thou art swift
To enter in the thoughts of desperate men!
I do remember an apothecary," &c.

This famous passage is so beautiful as to be self-justified; yet, in addition, what a fine preparation it is for the tomb scene!

Ib. sc. 3. Romeo's speech:—

"Good gentle youth, tempt not a desperate man,
Fly hence and leave me."

The gentleness of Romeo was shown before, as softened by love; and now it is doubled by love and sorrow and awe of the place where he is.

Ib. Romeo's speech:—

"How oft when men are at the point of death
Have they been merry! which their keepers call
A lightning before death. O, how may I
Call this a lightning?—-O, my love, my wife!" &c.

Here, here, is the master example how beauty can at once increase and modify passion!

Ib. Last scene.

How beautiful is the close! The spring and the winter meet;—winter assumes the character of spring, and spring the sadness of winter.

Shakespeare's English Historical Plays.

The first form of poetry is the epic, the essence of which may be stated as the successive in events and characters. This must be distinguished from narration, in which there must always be a narrator, from whom the objects represented receive a colouring and a manner;—whereas in the epic, as in the so-called poems of Homer, the whole is completely objective, and the representation is a pure reflection. The next form into which poetry passed was the dramatic;—both forms having a common basis with a certain difference, and that difference not consisting in the dialogue alone. Both are founded on the relation of providence to the human will; and this relation is the universal element, expressed under different points of view according to the difference of religion, and the moral and intellectual cultivation of different nations. In the epic poem fate is represented as overruling the will, and making it instrumental to the accomplishment of its designs:—

... Διὸς τελείετο βονλή

In the drama, the will is exhibited as struggling with fate, a great and beautiful instance and illustration of which is the Prometheus of Æschylus; and the deepest effect is produced when the fate is represented as a higher and intelligent will, and the opposition of the individual as springing from a defect.

In order that a drama may be properly historical, it is necessary that it should be the history of the people to whom it is addressed. In the composition, care must be taken that there appear no dramatic improbability, as the reality is taken for granted. It must, likewise, be poetical;—that only, I mean, must be taken which is the permanent in our nature, which is common, and therefore deeply interesting to all ages. The events themselves are immaterial, otherwise than as the clothing and manifestation of the spirit that is working within. In this mode, the unity resulting from succession is destroyed, but is supplied by a unity of a higher order, which connects the events by reference to the workers, gives a reason for them in the motives, and presents men in their causative character. It takes, therefore, that part of real history which is the least known, and infuses a principle of life and organisation into the naked facts, and makes them all the framework of an animated whole.

In my happier days, while I had yet hope and onward-looking thoughts, I planned an historical drama of King Stephen, in the manner of Shakespeare. Indeed, it would be desirable that some man of dramatic genius should dramatise all those omitted by Shakespeare, as far down as Henry VII. Perkin Warbeck would make a most interesting drama. A few scenes of Marlow's Edward II. might be preserved. After Henry VIII., the events are too well and distinctly known, to be, without plump inverisimilitude, crowded together in one night's exhibition. Whereas, the history of our ancient kings—the events of the reigns, I mean—are like stars in the sky;—whatever the real interspaces may be, and however great, they seem close to each other. The stars—the events—strike us and remain in our eye, little modified by the difference of dates. An historic drama is, therefore, a collection of events borrowed from history, but connected together in respect of cause and time, poetically and by dramatic fiction. It would be a fine national custom to act such a series of dramatic histories in orderly succession, in the yearly Christmas holidays, and could not but tend to counteract that mock cosmopolitism, which under a positive term really implies nothing but a negation of, or indifference to, the particular love of our country. By its nationality must every nation retain its independence;—I mean a nationality quoad the nation. Better thus;—nationality in each individual, quoad his country, is equal to the sense of individuality quoad himself; but himself as sub-sensuous and central. Patriotism is equal to the sense of individuality reflected from every other individual. There may come a higher virtue in both—just cosmopolitism. But this latter is not possible but by antecedence of the former.

Shakespeare has included the most important part of nine reigns in his historical dramas;— namely—King John, Richard II.—Henry IV. (two)—Henry V.—Henry VI. (three) including Edward V. and Henry VIII., in all ten plays. There remain, therefore, to be done, with the exception of a single scene or two that should be adopted from Marlow—eleven reigns—of which the first two appear the only unpromising subjects;—and those two dramas must be formed wholly or mainly of invented private stories, which, however, could not have happened except in consequence of the events and measures of these reigns, and which should furnish opportunity both of exhibiting the manners and oppressions of the times, and of narrating dramatically the great events;—if possible, the death of the two sovereigns, at least of the latter, should be made to have some influence on the finale of the story. All the rest are glorious subjects; especially Henry I. (being the struggle between the men of arms and of letters, in the persons of Henry and Becket), Stephen, Richard I., Edward II., and Henry VII.

"King John."

Act i. sc. 1.—

"Bast. James Gurney, wilt thou give us leave awhile?
Gur. Good leave, good Philip.
Bast. Philip? sparrow! James," &c.
Theobald adopts Warburton's conjecture of "spare me."

O true Warburton! and the sancta simplicitas of honest dull Theobald's faith in him! Nothing can be more lively or characteristic than "Philip? Sparrow!" Had Warburton read old Skelton's Philip Sparrow, an exquisite and original poem, and, no doubt, popular in Shakespeare's time, even Warburton would scarcely have made so deep a plunge into the bathetic as to have deathified "sparrow" into "spare me!"

Act iii. sc. 2. Speech of Faulconbridge:—

"Now, by my life, this day grows wondrous hot;
Some airy devil hovers in the sky," &c.
Theobald adopts Warburton's conjecture of "fiery."

I prefer the old text: the word "devil" implies "fiery." You need only read the line, laying a full and strong emphasis on "devil," to perceive the uselessness and tastelessness of Warburton's alteration.

"Richard II."

I have stated that the transitional link between the epic poem and the drama is the historic drama; that in the epic poem a pre-announced fate gradually adjusts and employs the will and the events as its instruments, whilst the drama, on the other hand, places fate and will in opposition to each other, and is then most perfect, when the victory of fate is obtained in consequence of imperfections in the opposing will, so as to leave a final impression that the fate itself is but a higher and a more intelligent will.

From the length of the speeches, and the circumstance that, with one exception, the events are all historical, and presented in their results, not produced by acts seen by, or taking place before, the audience, this tragedy is ill suited to our present large theatres. But in itself, and for the closet, I feel no hesitation in placing it as the first and most admirable of all Shakespeare's purely historical plays. For the two parts of Henry IV. form a species of themselves, which may be named the mixed drama. The distinction does not depend on the mere quantity of historical events in the play compared with the fictions; for there is as much history in Macbeth as in Richard, but in the relation of the history to the plot. In the purely historical plays, the history forms the plot; in the mixed, it directs it; in the rest, as Macbeth, Hamlet, Cymbeline, Lear, it subserves it. But, however unsuited to the stage this drama may be, God forbid that even there it should fall dead on the hearts of jacobinised

Englishmen! Then, indeed, we might say—præteriit gloria mundi! For the spirit of patriotic reminiscence is the all-permeating soul of this noble work. It is, perhaps, the most purely historical of Shakespeare's dramas. There are not in it, as in the others, characters introduced merely for the purpose of giving a greater individuality and realness, as in the comic parts of Henry IV., by presenting as it were our very selves. Shakespeare avails himself of every opportunity to effect the great object of the historic drama,—that, namely, of familiarising the people to the great names of their country, and thereby of exciting a steady patriotism, a love of just liberty, and a respect for all those fundamental institutions of social life, which bind men together:—

"This royal throne of kings, this sceptred isle,
This earth of majesty, this seat of Mars,
This other Eden, demi-paradise;
This fortress, built by nature for herself,
Against infection, and the hand of war;
This happy breed of men, this little world;
This precious stone set in the silver sea,
Which serves it in the office of a wall,
Or as a moat defensive to a home,
Against the envy of less happier lands;
This blessed plot, this earth, this realm, this England,
This nurse, this teeming womb of royal kings,
Fear'd by their breed, and famous by their birth," &c.
Add the famous passage in King John:—

"This England never did nor ever shall,
Lie at the proud foot of a conqueror,
But when it first did help to wound itself.
Now these her princes are come home again,
Come the three corners of the world in arms,
And we shall shock them: nought shall make us rue,
If England to itself do rest but true."

And it certainly seems that Shakespeare's historic dramas produced a very deep effect on the minds of the English people, and in earlier times they were familiar even to the least informed of all ranks, according to the relation of Bishop Corbett. Marlborough, we know, was not ashamed to confess that his principal acquaintance with English history was derived from them; and I believe that a large part of the information as to our old names and achievements even now abroad is due, directly or indirectly, to Shakespeare.

Admirable is the judgment with which Shakespeare always in the first scenes prepares, yet how naturally, and with what concealment of art, for the catastrophe. Observe how he here presents the germ of all the after events in Richard's insincerity, partiality, arbitrariness, and favouritism, and in the proud, tempestuous, temperament of his barons. In the very beginning, also, is displayed that feature in Richard's character, which is never forgotten throughout the play—his attention to decorum, and high feeling of the kingly dignity. These anticipations show with what judgment Shakespeare wrote, and illustrate his care to connect the past and the future, and unify them with the present by forecast and reminiscence.

It is interesting to a critical ear to compare the six opening lines of the play—

"Old John of Gaunt, time-honour'd Lancaster,
Hast thou, according to thy oath and band," &c.

each closing at the tenth syllable, with the rhythmless metre of the verse in Henry VI. and Titus Andronicus, in order that the difference, indeed, the heterogeneity, of the two may be felt etiam in simillimis prima superficie. Here the weight of the single words supplies all the relief afforded by intercurrent verse, while the whole represents the mood. And compare the apparently defective metre of Bolingbroke's first line—

"Many years of happy days befal"—
with Prospero's—

"Twelve years since, Miranda! twelve years since."
The actor should supply the time by emphasis, and pause on the first syllable of each of these verses.

Act i. sc. 1. Bolingbroke's speech:—

"First (heaven be the record to my speech!),
In the devotion of a subject's love," &c.
I remember in the Sophoclean drama no more striking example of the τὸ πρέπον καὶ σεμνὸν than this speech; and the rhymes in the last six lines well express the preconcertedness of Bolingbroke's scheme so beautifully contrasted with the vehemence and sincere irritation of Mowbray.

Ib. Bolingbroke's speech:—

"Which blood, like sacrificing Abel's, cries,
Even from the tongueless caverns of the earth,
To me, for justice and rough chastisement."
Note the δεινὸν of this "to me," which is evidently felt by Richard:—

"How high a pitch his resolution soars!"
and the affected depreciation afterwards;—

"As he is but my father's brother's son."
Ib. Mowbray's speech:—

"In haste whereof, most heartily I pray
Your highness to assign our trial day."

The occasional interspersion of rhymes, and the more frequent winding up of a speech therewith—what purpose was this designed to answer? In the earnest drama, I mean. Deliberateness? An attempt, as in Mowbray, to collect himself and be cool at the close?—I can see that in the following speeches the rhyme answers the end of the Greek chorus, and distinguishes the general truths from the passions of the dialogue; but this does not exactly justify the practice, which is unfrequent in proportion to the excellence of Shakespeare's plays. One thing, however, is to be observed,—that the speakers are historical, known, and so far formal characters, and their reality is already a fact. This should be borne in mind. The whole of this scene of the quarrel between Mowbray and Bolingbroke seems introduced for the purpose of showing by anticipation the characters of Richard and Bolingbroke. In the latter there is observable a decorous and courtly checking of his anger in subservience to a predetermined plan, especially in his calm speech after receiving sentence of banishment compared with Mowbray's unaffected lamentation. In the one, all is ambitious hope of something yet to come; in the other it is desolation and a looking backward of the heart,

Ib. sc. 2.—

"Gaunt. God's is the quarrel; for God's substitute,
His deputy anointed in his right,
Hath caus'd his death: the which, if wrongfully,
Let heaven revenge; for I may never lift
An angry arm against his minister."

Without the hollow extravagance of Beaumont and Fletcher's ultra-royalism, how carefully does Shakespeare acknowledge and reverence the eternal distinction between the mere individual, and the symbolic or representative, on which all genial law, no less than patriotism, depends. The whole of this second scene commences, and is anticipative of, the tone and character of the play at large.

Ib. sc. 3. In none of Shakespeare's fictitious dramas, or in those founded on a history as unknown to his auditors generally as fiction, is this violent rupture of the succession of time found:—a proof, I think, that the pure historic drama, like Richard II. and King John, had its own laws.

Ib. Mowbray's speech:—

"A dearer merit
Have I deserved at your highness' hand."
O, the instinctive propriety of Shakespeare in the choice of words!

Ib. Richard's speech:—

"Nor never by advised purpose meet,
To plot, contrive, or complot any ill,
'Gainst us, our state, our subjects, or our land."

Already the selfish weakness of Richard's character opens. Nothing will such minds so readily embrace, as indirect ways softened down to their quasi-consciences by policy, expedience, &c.

Ib. Mowbray's speech:—

... "All the world's my way."
"The world was all before him."—Milt.
Ib.—

"Boling. How long a time lies in one little word!
Four lagging winters, and four wanton springs,
End in a word: such is the breath of kings."
Admirable anticipation!

Ib. sc. 4. This is a striking conclusion of a first act,—letting the reader into the secret;—having before impressed us with the dignified and kingly manners of Richard, yet by well managed anticipations leading us on to the full gratification of pleasure in our own penetration. In this scene a new light is thrown on Richard's character. Until now he has appeared in all the beauty of royalty; but here, as soon as he is left to himself, the inherent weakness of his character is immediately shown. It is a weakness, however, of a peculiar kind, not arising from want of personal courage, or any specific defect of faculty, but rather an intellectual feminineness, which feels a necessity of ever leaning on the breasts of others, and of reclining on those who are all the while known to be inferiors. To this must be attributed as its consequences all Richard's vices, his tendency to concealment, and his cunning, the whole operation of which is directed to the getting rid of present difficulties. Richard is not meant to be a debauchee; but we see in him that sophistry which is common to man, by which we can deceive our own hearts, and at one and the same time apologize for, and yet commit, the error. Shakespeare has represented this character in a very peculiar manner. He has not made him amiable with counterbalancing faults; but has openly and broadly drawn those faults without reserve, relying on Richard's disproportionate sufferings and gradually emergent good qualities for our sympathy; and this was possible, because his faults are not positive vices, but spring entirely from defect of character.

Act ii. sc. 1.—

"K. Rich. Can sick men play so nicely with their names?"
Yes! on a death-bed there is a feeling which may make all things appear but as puns and equivocations. And a passion there is that carries off its own excess by plays on words as naturally, and, therefore, as appropriately to drama, as by gesticulations, looks, or tones. This belongs to human nature as such, independently of associations and habits from any particular rank of life or mode of employment; and in this consists Shakespeare's vulgarisms, as in Macbeth's—

"The devil damn thee black, thou cream-fac'd loon!" &c.
This is (to equivocate on Dante's words) in truth the nobile volgare eloquenza. Indeed it is profoundly true that there is a natural, an almost irresistible, tendency in the mind, when immersed in one strong feeling, to connect that feeling with every sight and object around it; especially if there be opposition, and the words addressed to it are in any way repugnant to the feeling itself, as here in the instance of Richard's unkind language:—

"Misery makes sport to mock itself."
No doubt, something of Shakespeare's punning must be attributed to his age, in which direct and formal combats of wit were a favourite pastime of the courtly and accomplished. It was an age more favourable, upon the whole, to vigour of intellect than the present, in which a dread of being thought pedantic dispirits and flattens the energies of original minds. But independently of this, I have no hesitation in saying that a pun, if it be congruous with the feeling of the scene, is not only allowable in the dramatic dialogue, but oftentimes one of the most effectual intensives of passion.

Ib.—

"K. Rich. Right; you say true, as Hereford's love, so his;
As theirs, so mine; and all be as it is."
The depth of this compared with the first scene:—

"How high a pitch," &c.

There is scarcely anything in Shakespeare in its degree, more admirably drawn than York's character; his religious loyalty struggling with a deep grief and indignation at the king's follies; his adherence to his word and faith, once given in spite of all, even the most natural, feelings. You see in him the weakness of old age, and the overwhelmingness of circumstances, for a time surmounting his sense of duty,—the junction of both exhibited in his boldness in words and feebleness in immediate act; and then again his effort to retrieve himself in abstract loyalty, even at the heavy price of the loss of his son. This species of accidental and adventitious weakness is brought into parallel with Richard's continually increasing energy of thought, and as constantly diminishing power of acting;—and thus it is Richard that breathes a harmony and a relation into all the characters of the play.

Ib. sc. 2.—

"Queen. To please the king I did; to please myself
I cannot do it; yet I know no cause
Why I should welcome such a guest as grief,
Save bidding farewell to so sweet a guest
As my sweet Richard: yet again, methinks,
Some unborn sorrow, ripe in sorrow's womb,
Is coming toward me; and my inward soul
With nothing trembles: at something it grieves,
More than with parting from my lord the king."

It is clear that Shakespeare never meant to represent Richard as a vulgar debauchee, but a man with a wantonness of spirit in external show, a feminine friendism, an intensity of woman-like love of those immediately about him, and a mistaking of the delight of being loved by him for a love of him. And mark in this scene Shakespeare's gentleness in touching the tender superstitions, the terræ incognitæ of presentiments, in the human mind; and how sharp a line of distinction he commonly draws between these obscure forecastings of general experience in each individual, and the vulgar errors of mere tradition. Indeed, it may be taken once for all as the truth, that Shakespeare, in the absolute universality of his genius, always reverences whatever arises out of our moral nature; he never profanes his muse with a contemptuous reasoning away of the genuine and general, however unaccountable, feelings of mankind.

The amiable part of Richard's character is brought full upon us by his queen's few words—

... "So sweet a guest
As my sweet Richard:"—

and Shakespeare has carefully shown in him an intense love of his country, well-knowing how that feeling would, in a pure historic drama, redeem him in the hearts of the audience. Yet even in this love there is something feminine and personal:—

"Dear earth, I do salute thee with my hand,—
As a long parted mother with her child
Plays fondly with her tears, and smiles in meeting;
So weeping, smiling, greet I thee, my earth,
And do thee favour with my royal hands."

With this is combined a constant overflow of emotions from a total incapability of controlling them, and thence a waste of that energy, which should have been reserved for actions, in the passion and effort of mere resolves and menaces. The consequence is moral exhaustion, and rapid alternations of unmanly despair and ungrounded hope,—every feeling being abandoned for its direct opposite upon the pressure of external accident. And yet when Richard's inward weakness appears to seek refuge in his despair, and his exhaustion counterfeits repose, the old habit of kingliness, the effect of flatterers from his infancy, is ever and anon producing in him a sort of wordy courage which only serves to betray more clearly his internal impotence. The second and third scenes of the third act combine and illustrate all this:—

"Aumerle. He means, my lord, that we are too remiss;
Whilst Bolingbroke, through our security,
Grows strong and great, in substance, and in friends.
K. Rich. Discomfortable cousin! know'st thou not,
That when the searching eye of heaven is hid
Behind the globe, that lights the lower world,
Then thieves and robbers range abroad unseen,
In murders and in outrage, bloody here;
But when, from under this terrestrial ball,
He fires the proud tops of the eastern pines,
And darts his light through every guilty hole,
Then murders, treasons, and detested sins,
The cloke of night being pluckt from off their backs,
Stand bare and naked, trembling at themselves?
So when this thief, this traitor, Bolingbroke, &c.
Aumerle. Where is the Duke my father with his power?
K. Rich. No matter where; of comfort no man speak:
Let's talk of graves, of worms, and epitaphs,
Make dust our paper, and with rainy eyes
Write sorrow on the bosom of the earth, &c.
Aumerle. My father hath a power, enquire of him;
And learn to make a body of a limb.
K. Rich. Thou chid'st me well: proud Bolingbroke, I come
To change blows with thee for our day of doom.
This ague-fit of fear is over-blown;
An easy task it is to win our own.
Scroop. Your uncle York hath join'd with Bolingbroke.—
K. Rich. Thou hast said enough,
Beshrew thee, cousin, which didst lead me forth
Of that sweet way I was in to despair!
What say you now? what comfort have we now?
By heaven, I'll hate him everlastingly,
That bids me be of comfort any more."
Act iii. sc. 3. Bolingbroke's speech:—

"Noble lord,
Go to the rude ribs of that ancient castle," &c.

Observe the fine struggle of a haughty sense of power and ambition in Bolingbroke with the necessity for dissimulation.

Ib. sc. 4. See here the skill and judgment of our poet in giving reality and individual life, by the introduction of accidents in his historic plays, and thereby making them dramas, and not histories. How beautiful an islet of repose—a melancholy repose, indeed—is this scene with the Gardener and his Servant. And how truly affecting and realising is the incident of the very horse Barbary, in the scene with the Groom in the last act!—

"Groom. I was a poor groom of thy stable, King,
When thou wert King; who, travelling towards York,

With much ado, at length have gotten leave
To look upon my sometimes master's face.
O, how it yearn'd my heart, when I beheld,
In London streets, that coronation day,
When Bolingbroke rode on roan Barbary!
That horse, that thou so often hast bestrid;
That horse, that I so carefully have dress'd!
K. Rich. Rode he on Barbary?"

Bolingbroke's character, in general, is an instance how Shakespeare makes one play introductory to another; for it is evidently a preparation for Henry IV., as Gloster in the third part of Henry VI. is for Richard III.

I would once more remark upon the exalted idea of the only true loyalty developed in this noble and impressive play. We have neither the rants of Beaumont and Fletcher, nor the sneers of Massinger;—the vast importance of the personal character of the sovereign is distinctly enounced, whilst, at the same time, the genuine sanctity which surrounds him is attributed to, and grounded on, the position in which he stands as the convergence and exponent of the life and power of the state.

The great end of the body politic appears to be to humanise, and assist in the progressiveness of, the animal man;—but the problem is so complicated with contingencies as to render it nearly impossible to lay down rules for the formation of a state. And should we be able to form a system of government, which should so balance its different powers as to form a check upon each, and so continually remedy and correct itself, it would, nevertheless, defeat its own aim;—for man is destined to be guided by higher principles, by universal views, which can never be fulfilled in this state of existence,—by a spirit of progressiveness which can never be accomplished, for then it would cease to be. Plato's Republic is like Bunyan's Town of Man-Soul,—a description of an individual, all of whose faculties are in their proper subordination and inter-dependence; and this it is assumed may be the prototype of the state as one great individual. But there is this sophism in it, that it is forgotten that the human faculties, indeed, are parts and not separate things; but that you could never get chiefs who were wholly reason, ministers who were wholly understanding, soldiers all wrath, labourers all concupiscence, and so on through the rest. Each of these partakes of, and interferes with, all the others.

"Henry IV.—Part I."

Act i. sc. 1. King Henry's speech:—

"No more the thirsty entrance of this soil
Shall daub her lips with her own children's blood."

A most obscure passage: but I think Theobald's interpretation right, namely, that "thirsty entrance" means the dry penetrability, or bibulous drought, of the soil. The obscurity of this passage is of the Shakesperian sort.

Ib. sc. 2. In this, the first introduction of Falstaff, observe the consciousness and the intentionality of his wit, so that when it does not flow of its own accord, its absence is felt, and an effort visibly made to recall it. Note also throughout how Falstaff's pride is gratified in the power of influencing a prince of the blood, the heir apparent, by means of it. Hence his dislike to Prince John of Lancaster, and his mortification when he finds his wit fail on him:—

"P. John. Fare you well, Falstaff: I, in my condition,
Shall better speak of you than you deserve.
Fal. I would you had but the wit; 'twere better than your
dukedom.—Good faith, this same young sober-blooded boy doth
not love me;—nor a man cannot make him laugh."
Act ii. sc. 1. Second Carrier's speech:—

... "breeds fleas like a loach."
Perhaps it is a misprint, or a provincial pronunciation, for "leach," that is, blood-suckers. Had it been gnats, instead of fleas, there might have been some sense, though small probability, in Warburton's suggestion of the Scottish "loch." Possibly "loach," or "lutch," may be some lost word for dovecote, or poultry-lodge, notorious for breeding fleas. In Stevens's or my reading, it should properly be "loaches," or "leeches," in the plural; except that I think I have heard anglers speak of trouts like a salmon.

Act iii. sc. 1.—

"Glend. Nay, if you melt, then will she run mad."
This "nay" so to be dwelt on in speaking, as to be equivalent to a dissyllable - u, is characteristic of the solemn Glendower; but the imperfect line

"She bids you
Upon the wanton rushes lay you down," &c.,
is one of those fine hair-strokes of exquisite judgment peculiar to Shakespeare;—thus detaching the Lady's speech, and giving it the individuality and entireness of a little poem, while he draws attention to it.

"Henry IV.—Part II."

Act ii. sc. 2—

"P. Hen. Sup any women with him?
Page. None, my lord, but old mistress Quickly, and mistress
Doll Tear-sheet.
P. Hen. This Doll Tear-sheet should be some road."
I am sometimes disposed to think that this respectable young lady's name is a very old corruption for Tear-street—street-walker, terere stratam (viam). Does not the Prince's question rather show this?—

"This Doll Tear-street should be some road?"
Act iii. sc. 1. King Henry's speech:—

... "Then, happy low, lie down;
Uneasy lies the head that wears a crown."
I know no argument by which to persuade any one to be of my opinion, or rather of my feeling; but yet I cannot help feeling that "Happy low-lie-down!" is either a proverbial expression, or the burthen of some old song, and means, "Happy the man, who lays himself down on his straw bed or chaff pallet on the ground or floor!"

Ib. sc. 2. Shallow's speech:—

"Rah, tah, tah, would 'a say; bounce, would 'a say," &c.

That Beaumont and Fletcher have more than once been guilty of sneering at their great master, cannot, I fear, be denied; but the passage quoted by Theobald from the Knight of the Burning Pestle is an imitation. If it be chargeable with any fault, it is with plagiarism, not with sarcasm.

"Henry V."

Act i. sc. 2. Westmoreland's speech:—

"They know your grace hath cause, and means, and might;
So hath your highness; never King of England
Had nobles richer," &c.

Does "grace" mean the king's own peculiar domains and legal revenue, and "highness" his feudal rights in the military service of his nobles?—I have sometimes thought it possible that the words "grace" and "cause" may have been transposed in the copying or printing;—

"They know your cause hath grace," &c.

What Theobald meant, I cannot guess. To me his pointing makes the passage still more obscure. Perhaps the lines ought to be recited dramatically thus:—

"They know your Grace hath cause, and means, and might:—
So hath your Highness—never King of England
Had nobles richer," &c.

He breaks off from the grammar and natural order from earnestness, and in order to give the meaning more passionately.

Ib. Exeter's speech:—

"Yet that is but a crush'd necessity."

Perhaps it may be "crash" for "crass" from crassus, clumsy; or it may be "curt," defective, imperfect: anything would be better than Warburton's "'scus'd," which honest Theobald, of course, adopts. By the by, it seems clear to me that this speech of Exeter's properly belongs to Canterbury, and was altered by the actors for convenience.

Act iv. sc. 3. King Henry's speech:—

"We would not die in that man's company
That fears his fellowship to die with us."

Should it not be "live" in the first line?

Ib. sc. 5.—

"Const. O diable!
Orl. O seigneur! le jour est perdu, tout est perdu!
Dan. Mort de ma vie! all is confounded, all!
Reproach and everlasting shame
Sit mocking in our plumes!—O meschante fortune!
Do not run away!"

Ludicrous as these introductory scraps of French appear, so instantly followed by good, nervous mother-English, yet they are judicious, and produce the impression which

Shakespeare intended,—a sudden feeling struck at once on the ears, as well as the eyes, of the audience, that "here come the French, the baffled French braggards!"—And this will appear still more judicious, when we reflect on the scanty apparatus of distinguishing dresses in Shakespeare's tyring-room.

"Henry VI.—Part I."

Act i. sc. 1. Bedford's speech:—

"Hung be the heavens with black, yield day to night!
Comets, importing change of times and states,
Brandish your crystal tresses in the sky;
And with them scourge the bad revolting stars
That have consented unto Henry's death!
Henry the fifth, too famous to live long!
England ne'er lost a king of so much worth."
Read aloud any two or three passages in blank verse even from Shakespeare's earliest dramas, as Love's Labour's Lost, or Romeo and Juliet; and then read in the same way this speech, with especial attention to the metre; and if you do not feel the impossibility of the latter having been written by Shakespeare, all I dare suggest is, that you may have ears,—for so has another animal,—but an ear you cannot have, me judice.

"Richard III."

This play should be contrasted with Richard II. Pride of intellect is the characteristic of Richard, carried to the extent of even boasting to his own mind of his villany, whilst others are present to feed his pride of superiority; as in his first speech, act ii. sc. 1. Shakespeare here, as in all his great parts, developes in a tone of sublime morality the dreadful consequences of placing the moral, in subordination to the mere intellectual, being. In Richard there is a predominance of irony, accompanied with apparently blunt manners to those immediately about him, but formalised into a more set hypocrisy towards the people as represented by their magistrates.

"Lear."

Of all Shakespeare's plays Macbeth is the most rapid, Hamlet the slowest, in movement. Lear combines length with rapidity,—like the hurricane and the whirlpool, absorbing while it advances. It begins as a stormy day in summer, with brightness; but that brightness is lurid, and anticipates the tempest.

It was not without forethought, nor is it without its due significance, that the division of Lear's kingdom is in the first six lines of the play stated as a thing already determined in all its particulars, previously to the trial of professions, as the relative rewards of which the daughters were to be made to consider their several portions. The strange, yet by no means unnatural, mixture of selfishness, sensibility, and habit of feeling derived from, and fostered by, the particular rank and usages of the individual;—the intense desire of being intensely beloved,—selfish, and yet characteristic of the selfishness of a loving and kindly nature alone;—the self-supportless leaning for all pleasure on another's breast;—the craving after sympathy with a prodigal disinterestedness, frustrated by its own ostentation, and the mode and nature of its claims;—the anxiety, the distrust, the jealousy, which more or less accompany all selfish affections, and are amongst the surest contradistinctions of mere fondness from true love, and which originate Lear's eager wish to enjoy his daughter's violent professions, whilst the inveterate habits of sovereignty convert the wish into claim and positive right, and an incompliance with it into crime and treason;—these facts, these passions, these moral verities, on which the whole tragedy is founded, are all prepared for, and will to the retrospect be found implied, in these first four or five lines of the play. They let us know that the trial is but a trick; and that the grossness of the old king's rage is in part the natural result of a silly trick suddenly and most unexpectedly baffled and disappointed.

It may here be worthy of notice, that Lear is the only serious performance of Shakespeare, the interest and situations of which are derived from the assumption of a gross improbability; whereas Beaumont and Fletcher's tragedies are, almost all of them, founded on some out of the way accident or exception to the general experience of mankind. But observe the matchless judgment of our Shakespeare. First, improbable as the conduct of Lear is in the first scene, yet it was an old story rooted in the popular faith,—a thing taken for granted already, and consequently without any of the effects of improbability. Secondly, it is merely the canvass for the characters and passions,—a mere occasion for,—and not, in the manner of Beaumont and Fletcher, perpetually recurring as the cause, and sine qua non of,—the incidents and emotions. Let the first scene of this play have been lost, and let it only be understood that a fond father had been duped by hypocritical professions of love and duty on the part of two daughters to disinherit the third, previously, and deservedly, more dear to him;—and all the rest of the tragedy would retain its interest undiminished, and be perfectly intelligible.

The accidental is nowhere the groundwork of the passions, but that which is catholic, which in all ages has been, and ever will be, close and native to the heart of man,—parental anguish from filial ingratitude, the genuineness of worth, though coffined in bluntness, and the execrable vileness of a smooth iniquity. Perhaps I ought to have added the Merchant of Venice; but here too the same remarks apply. It was an old tale; and substitute any other danger than that of the pound of flesh (the circumstance in which the improbability lies), yet all the situations and the emotions appertaining to them remain equally excellent and appropriate. Whereas take away from the Mad Lover of Beaumont and Fletcher the fantastic hypothesis of his engagement to cut out his own heart, and have it presented to his mistress, and all the main scenes must go with it.

Kotzebue is the German Beaumont and Fletcher, without their poetic powers, and without their vis comica. But, like them, he always deduces his situations and passions from marvellous accidents, and the trick of bringing one part of our moral nature to counteract another; as our pity for misfortune and admiration of generosity and courage to combat our condemnation of guilt as in adultery, robbery, and other heinous crimes;—and, like them too, he excels in his mode of telling a story clearly and interestingly, in a series of dramatic dialogues. Only the trick of making tragedy-heroes and heroines out of shopkeepers and barmaids was too low for the age, and too unpoetic for the genius, of Beaumont and Fletcher, inferior in every respect as they are to their great predecessor and contemporary. How inferior would they have appeared, had not Shakespeare existed for them to imitate;—which in every play, more or less, they do, and in their tragedies most glaringly:—and yet—(O shame! shame!)—they miss no opportunity of sneering at the divine man, and sub-detracting from his merits!

To return to Lear. Having thus in the fewest words, and in a natural reply to as natural a question,—which yet answers the secondary purpose of attracting our attention to the difference or diversity between the characters of Cornwall and Albany,—provided the prémisses and data, as it were, for our after insight into the mind and mood of the person, whose character, passions, and sufferings are the main subject-matter of the play;—from Lear, the persona patiens of his drama, Shakespeare passes without delay to the second in importance, the chief agent and prime mover, and introduces Edmund to our acquaintance, preparing us with the same felicity of judgment, and in the same easy and natural way, for his character in the seemingly casual communication of its origin and occasion. From the first drawing up of the curtain Edmund has stood before us in the united strength and beauty of earliest manhood. Our eyes have been questioning him. Gifted as he is with high advantages of person, and further endowed by nature with a powerful intellect and a strong energetic will, even without any concurrence of circumstances and accident, pride will necessarily be the sin that most easily besets him. But Edmund is also the known and acknowledged son of the princely Gloster: he, therefore, has both the germ of pride, and the conditions best fitted to evolve and ripen it into a predominant feeling. Yet hitherto no reason appears why it should be other than the not unusual pride of person, talent, and birth,—a pride auxiliary, if not akin, to many virtues, and the natural ally of honourable impulses. But alas! in his own presence his own father takes shame to himself for the frank avowal that he is his father,—he has "blushed so often to acknowledge him that he is now brazed to it!" Edmund hears the circumstances of his birth spoken of with a most degrading and licentious levity,—his mother described as a wanton by her own paramour, and the remembrance of the animal sting, the low criminal gratifications connected with her wantonness and prostituted beauty, assigned as the reason why "the whoreson must be acknowledged!" This, and the consciousness of its notoriety; the gnawing conviction that every show of respect is an effort of courtesy, which recalls, while it represses, a contrary feeling;—this is the ever trickling flow of wormwood and gall into the wounds of pride,—the corrosive virus which inoculates pride with a venom not its own, with envy, hatred, and a lust for that power which in its blaze of radiance would hide the dark spots on his disc,—with pangs of shame personally undeserved, and therefore felt as wrongs, and with a blind ferment of vindictive working towards the occasions and causes, especially towards a brother, whose stainless birth and lawful honours were the constant remembrancers of his own debasement, and were ever in the way to prevent all chance of its being unknown, or overlooked and forgotten. Add to this, that with excellent judgment, and provident for the claims of the moral sense,—for that which, relatively to the drama, is called poetic justice, and as the fittest means for reconciling the feelings of the spectators to the horrors of Gloster's after sufferings,—at least, of rendering them somewhat less unendurable—(for I will not disguise my conviction, that in this one point the tragic in this play has been urged beyond the outermost mark and ne plus ultra of the dramatic);—Shakespeare has precluded all excuse and palliation of the guilt incurred by both the parents of the base-born Edmund, by Gloster's confession that he was at the time a married man, and already blest with a lawful heir of his fortunes. The mournful alienation of brotherly love, occasioned by the law of primogeniture in noble families, or rather by the unnecessary distinctions engrafted thereon, and this in children of the same stock, is still almost proverbial on the continent,—especially, as I know from my own observation, in the south of Europe,—and appears to have been scarcely less common in our own island before the Revolution of 1688, if we may judge from the characters and sentiments so frequent in our elder comedies. There is the younger brother, for instance, in Beaumont and Fletcher's play of the Scornful Lady, on the one side, and Oliver in Shakespeare's As You Like It, on the other. Need it be said how heavy an aggravation, in such a case, the stain of bastardy must have been, were it only that the younger brother was liable to hear his own dishonour and his mother's infamy related by his father with an excusing shrug of the shoulders, and in a tone betwixt waggery and shame!

By the circumstances here enumerated as so many predisposing causes, Edmund's character might well be deemed already sufficiently explained; and our minds prepared for it. But in this tragedy the story or fable constrained Shakespeare to introduce wickedness in an outrageous form in the persons of Regan and Goneril. He had read nature too heedfully not to know that courage, intellect, and strength of character are the most impressive forms of power, and that to power in itself, without reference to any moral end, an inevitable admiration and complacency appertains, whether it be displayed in the conquests of a Buonaparte or Tamerlane, or in the foam and the thunder of a cataract. But in the exhibition of such a character it was of the highest importance to prevent the guilt from passing into utter monstrosity,—which again depends on the presence or absence of causes and temptations sufficient to account for the wickedness, without the necessity of recurring to a thorough fiendishness of nature for its origination. For such are the appointed relations of intellectual power to truth, and of truth to goodness, that it becomes both morally and poetically unsafe to present what is admirable—what our nature compels us to admire—in the mind, and what is most detestable in the heart, as co-existing in the same individual without any apparent connection, or any modification of the one by the other. That Shakespeare has in one instance, that of Iago, approached to this, and that he has done it successfully, is perhaps the most astonishing proof of his genius, and the opulence of its resources. But in the present tragedy, in which he was compelled to present a Goneril and a Regan, it was most carefully to be avoided;—and therefore the only one conceivable addition to the inauspicious influences on the preformation of Edmund's character is given, in the information that all the kindly counteractions to the mischievous feelings of shame, which might have been derived from co-domestication with Edgar and their common father, had been cut off by his absence from home, and foreign education from boyhood to the present time, and a prospect of its continuance, as if to preclude all risk of his interference with the father's views for the elder and legitimate son:—

"He hath been out nine years, and away he shall again."
Act i. sc. 1.—

"Cor. Nothing my lord.
Lear. Nothing?
Cor. Nothing.
Lear. Nothing can come of nothing: speak again.
Cor. Unhappy that I am, I cannot heave
My heart into my mouth: I love your majesty
According to my bond; nor more, nor less."

There is something of disgust at the ruthless hypocrisy of her sisters, and some little faulty admixture of pride and sullenness in Cordelia's "Nothing;" and her tone is well contrived, indeed, to lessen the glaring absurdity of Lear's conduct, but answers the yet more important purpose of forcing away the attention from the nursery-tale, the moment it has served its end, that of supplying the canvas for the picture. This is also materially furthered by Kent's opposition, which displays Lear's moral incapability of resigning the sovereign power in the very act of disposing of it. Kent is, perhaps, the nearest to perfect goodness in all Shakespeare's characters, and yet the most individualised. There is an extraordinary charm, in his bluntness, which is that only of a nobleman, arising from a contempt of overstrained courtesy, and combined with easy placability where goodness of heart is apparent. His passionate affection for, and fidelity to, Lear act on our feelings in Lear's own favour: virtue itself seems to be in company with him.

Ib. sc. 2. Edmund's speech:—

"Who, in the lusty stealth of nature, take
More composition and fierce quality
Than doth," &c.
Warburton's note upon a quotation from Vanini.

Poor Vanini!—Any one but Warburton would have thought this precious passage more characteristic of Mr. Shandy than of atheism. If the fact really were so (which it is not, but almost the contrary) I do not see why the most confirmed theist might not very naturally utter the same wish. But it is proverbial that the youngest son in a large family is commonly the man of the greatest talents in it; and as good an authority as Vanini has said—"incalescere in venerem ardentius, spei sobolis injuriosum esse."

In this speech of Edmund you see, as soon as a man cannot reconcile himself to reason, how his conscience flies off by way of appeal to nature, who is sure upon such occasions never to find fault, and also how shame sharpens a predisposition in the heart to evil. For it is a profound moral, that shame will naturally generate guilt; the oppressed will be vindictive, like Shylock, and in the anguish of undeserved ignominy the delusion secretly springs up of getting over the moral quality of an action by fixing the mind on the mere physical act alone.

Ib. Edmund's speech:—

"This is the excellent foppery of the world! that, when we are sick in fortune (often the surfeit of our own behaviour), we make guilty of our disasters, the sun, the moon, and the stars," &c.

Thus scorn and misanthropy are often the anticipations and mouth-pieces of wisdom in the detection of superstitions. Both individuals and nations may be free from such prejudices by being below them, as well as by rising above them.

Ib. sc. 3. The Steward should be placed in exact antithesis to Kent, as the only character of utter irredeemable baseness in Shakespeare. Even in this the judgment and invention of the poet are very observable;—for what else could the willing tool of a Goneril be? Not a vice but this of baseness was left open to him.

Ib. sc. 4. In Lear old age is itself a character,—its natural imperfections being increased by life-long habits of receiving a prompt obedience. Any addition of individuality would have been unnecessary and painful; for the relations of others to him, of wondrous fidelity and of frightful ingratitude, alone sufficiently distinguish him. Thus Lear becomes the open and ample play-room of nature's passions.

Ib.—

"Knight. Since my young lady's going into France, Sir; the
fool hath much pined away."
The Fool is no comic buffoon to make the groundlings laugh,—no forced condescension of Shakespeare's genius to the taste of his audience. Accordingly the poet prepares for his introduction, which he never does with any of his common clowns and fools, by bringing him into living connection with the pathos of the play. He is as wonderful a creation as Caliban;—his wild babblings, and inspired idiocy, articulate and gauge the horrors of the scene.

The monster Goneril prepares what is necessary, while the character of Albany renders a still more maddening grievance possible—namely, Regan and Cornwall in perfect sympathy of monstrosity. Not a sentiment, not an image, which can give pleasure on its own account is admitted; whenever these creatures are introduced, and they are brought forward as little as possible, pure horror reigns throughout. In this scene and in all the early speeches of Lear, the one general sentiment of filial ingratitude prevails as the main-spring of the feelings;—in this early stage the outward object causing the pressure on the mind, which is not yet sufficiently familiarised with the anguish for the imagination to work upon it.

Ib.—

"Gon. Do you mark that, my lord?
Alb. I cannot be so partial, Goneril,
To the great love I bear you.
Gon. Pray you content," &c.
Observe the baffled endeavour of Goneril to act on the fears of Albany, and yet his passiveness, his inertia; he is not convinced, and yet he is afraid of looking into the thing. Such characters always yield to those who will take the trouble of governing them, or for them. Perhaps the influence of a princess, whose choice of him had royalised his state, may be some little excuse for Albany's weakness.

Ib. sc. 5.—

"Lear. O let me not be mad, not mad, sweet heaven!
Keep me in temper! I would not be mad!"
The mind's own anticipation of madness! The deepest tragic notes are often struck by a half sense of an impending blow. The Fool's conclusion of this act by a grotesque prattling seems to indicate the dislocation of feeling that has begun and is to be continued.

Act ii. sc. 1. Edmund's speech:—

... "He replied,
Thou unpossessing bastard!" &c.
Thus the secret poison in Edmund's own heart steals forth; and then observe poor Gloster's—

"Loyal and natural boy!"—
as if praising the crime of Edmund's birth!

Ib. Compare Regan's—

"What, did my father's godson seek your life?
He whom my father named?"—
with the unfeminine violence of her—

"All vengeance comes too short," &c.—
and yet no reference to the guilt, but only to the accident, which she uses as an occasion for sneering at her father. Regan is not, in fact, a greater monster than Goneril, but she has the power of casting more venom.

Ib. sc. 2. Cornwall's speech:—

... "This is some fellow,
Who, having been praised for bluntness, doth affect
A saucy roughness," &c.

In thus placing these profound general truths in the mouths of such men as Cornwall, Edmund, Iago, &c., Shakespeare at once gives them utterance, and yet shows how indefinite their application is.

Ib. sc. 3. Edgar's assumed madness serves the great purpose of taking off part of the shock which would otherwise be caused by the true madness of Lear, and further displays the profound difference between the two. In every attempt at representing madness throughout the whole range of dramatic literature, with the single exception of Lear, it is mere lightheadedness, as especially in Otway. In Edgar's ravings Shakespeare all the while lets you see a fixed purpose, a practical end in view;—in Lear's, there is only the brooding of the one anguish, an eddy without progression.

Ib. sc. 4. Lear's speech:—

"The king would speak with Cornwall; the dear father
Would with his daughter speak, &c.
No, but not yet: may be he is not well," &c.

The strong interest now felt by Lear to try to find excuses for his daughter is most pathetic.

Ib. Lear's speech:—

... "Beloved Regan,
Thy sister's naught;—O Regan, she hath tied
Sharp-tooth'd unkindness, like a vulture, here.
I can scarce speak to thee;—thou'lt not believe
Of how deprav'd a quality—O Regan!
Reg. I pray you, Sir, take patience; I have hope,
You less know how to value her desert,
Than she to scant her duty.
Lear. Say, how is that?"

Nothing is so heart-cutting as a cold unexpected defence or palliation of a cruelty passionately complained of, or so expressive of thorough hard-heartedness. And feel the excessive horror of Regan's "O, Sir, you are old!"—and then her drawing from that universal object of reverence and indulgence the very reason for her frightful conclusion—

"Say, you have wrong'd her!"

All Lear's faults increase our pity for him. We refuse to know them otherwise than as means of his sufferings, and aggravations of his daughters' ingratitude.

Ib. Lear's speech:—

"O, reason not the need: our basest beggars
Are in the poorest thing superfluous," &c.

Observe that the tranquillity which follows the first stunning of the blow permits Lear to reason.

Act iii. sc. 4. O, what a world's convention of agonies is here! All external nature in a storm, all moral nature convulsed,—the real madness of Lear, the feigned madness of Edgar, the babbling of the Fool, the desperate fidelity of Kent—surely such a scene was never conceived before or since! Take it but as a picture for the eye only, it is more terrific than any which a Michael Angelo, inspired by a Dante, could have conceived, and which none but a Michael Angelo could have executed. Or let it have been uttered to the blind, the howlings of nature would seem converted into the voice of conscious humanity. This scene ends with the first symptoms of positive derangement; and the intervention of the fifth scene is particularly judicious,—the interruption allowing an interval for Lear to appear in full madness in the sixth scene.

Ib. sc. 7. Gloster's blinding.

What can I say of this scene?—There is my reluctance to think Shakespeare wrong, and yet—

Act iv. sc. 6. Lear's speech:—

"Ha! Goneril!—with a white beard!—They flattered me like a dog; and told me, I had white hairs in my beard, ere the black ones were there. To say Ay and No to every thing I said!—Ay and No too was no good divinity. When the rain came to wet me once," &c.
The thunder recurs, but still at a greater distance from our feelings.

Ib. sc. 7. Lear's speech:—

"Where have I been? Where am I?—Fair daylight?—
I am mightily abused.—I should even die with pity
To see another thus," &c.
How beautifully the affecting return of Lear to reason, and the mild pathos of these speeches prepare the mind for the last sad, yet sweet, consolation of the aged sufferer's death!

"Hamlet."

Hamlet was the play, or rather Hamlet himself was the character, in the intuition and exposition of which I first made my turn for philosophical criticism, and especially for insight into the genius of Shakespeare, noticed. This happened first amongst my acquaintances, as Sir George Beaumont will bear witness; and subsequently, long before Schlegel had delivered at Vienna the lectures on Shakespeare, which he afterwards published, I had given on the same subject eighteen lectures substantially the same, proceeding from the very same point of view, and deducing the same conclusions, so far as I either then agreed, or now agree, with him. I gave these lectures at the Royal Institution, before six or seven hundred auditors of rank and eminence, in the spring of the same year, in which Sir Humphrey Davy, a fellow-lecturer, made his great revolutionary discoveries in chemistry. Even in detail the coincidence of Schlegel with my lectures was so extraordinary, that all who at a later period heard the same words, taken by me from my notes of the lectures at the Royal Institution, concluded a borrowing on my part from Schlegel. Mr. Hazlitt, whose hatred of me is in such an inverse ratio to my zealous kindness towards him, as to be defended by his warmest admirer, Charles Lamb—(who, God bless him! besides his characteristic obstinacy of adherence to old friends, as long at least as they are at all down in the world, is linked as by a charm to Hazlitt's conversation)—only as "frantic;"—Mr. Hazlitt, I say, himself replied to an assertion of my plagiarism from Schlegel in these words;—"That is a lie; for I myself heard the very same character of Hamlet from Coleridge before he went to Germany, and when he had neither read nor could read a page of German!" Now Hazlitt was on a visit to me at my cottage at Nether Stowey, Somerset, in the summer of the year 1798, in the September of which year I first was out of sight of the shores of Great Britain.—Recorded by me, S. T. Coleridge, 7th January, 1819.

The seeming inconsistencies in the conduct and character of Hamlet have long exercised the conjectural ingenuity of critics; and, as we are always loth to suppose that the cause of defective apprehension is in ourselves, the mystery has been too commonly explained by the very easy process of setting it down as in fact inexplicable, and by resolving the phenomenon into a misgrowth or lusus of the capricious and irregular genius of Shakespeare. The shallow and stupid arrogance of these vulgar and indolent decisions I would fain do my best to expose. I believe the character of Hamlet may be traced to Shakespeare's deep and accurate science in mental philosophy. Indeed, that this character must have some connection with the common fundamental laws of our nature may be assumed from the fact, that Hamlet has been the darling of every country in which the literature of England has been fostered. In order to understand him, it is essential that we should reflect on the constitution of our own minds. Man is distinguished from the brute animals in proportion as thought prevails over sense: but in the healthy processes of the mind, a balance is constantly maintained between the impressions from outward objects and the inward operations of the intellect;—for if there be an overbalance in the contemplative faculty, man thereby becomes the creature of mere meditation, and loses his natural power of action. Now one of Shakespeare's modes of creating characters is, to conceive any one intellectual or moral faculty in morbid excess, and then to place himself, Shakespeare, thus mutilated or diseased, under given circumstances. In Hamlet he seems to have wished to exemplify the moral necessity of a due balance between our attention to the objects of our senses, and our meditation on the workings of our minds,—an equilibrium between the real and the imaginary worlds. In Hamlet this balance is disturbed: his thoughts, and the images of his fancy, are far more vivid than his actual perceptions, and his very perceptions, instantly passing through the medium of his contemplations, acquire, as they pass, a form and a colour not naturally their own. Hence we see a great, an almost enormous, intellectual activity, and a proportionate aversion to real action, consequent upon it, with all its symptoms and accompanying qualities. This character Shakespeare places in circumstances, under which it is obliged to act on the spur of the moment:—Hamlet is brave and careless of death; but he vacillates from sensibility, and procrastinates from thought, and loses the power of action in the energy of resolve. Thus it is that this tragedy presents a direct contrast to that of Macbeth; the one proceeds with the utmost slowness, the other with a crowded and breathless rapidity.

The effect of this overbalance of the imaginative power is beautifully illustrated in the everlasting broodings and superfluous activities of Hamlet's mind, which, unseated from its healthy relation, is constantly occupied with the world within, and abstracted from the world without,—giving substance to shadows, and throwing a mist over all commonplace actualities. It is the nature of thought to be indefinite;—definiteness belongs to external imagery alone. Hence it is that the sense of sublimity arises, not from the sight of an outward object, but from the beholder's reflection upon it;—not from the sensuous impression, but from the imaginative reflex. Few have seen a celebrated waterfall without feeling something akin to disappointment: it is only subsequently that the image comes back full into the mind, and brings with it a train of grand or beautiful associations. Hamlet feels this; his senses are in a state of trance, and he looks upon external things as hieroglyphics. His soliloquy—

"O! that this too too solid flesh would melt," &c.—

springs from that craving after the indefinite—for that which is not—which most easily besets men of genius; and the self-delusion common to this temper of mind is finely exemplified in the character which Hamlet gives of himself;—

... "It cannot be
But I am pigeon-liver'd, and lack gall
To make oppression bitter."
He mistakes the seeing his chains for the breaking them, delays action till action is of no use, and dies the victim of mere circumstance and accident.

There is a great significancy in the names of Shakespeare's plays. In the Twelfth Night, Midsummer Night's Dream, As You Like It, and Winter's Tale, the total effect is produced by a co-ordination of the characters as in a wreath of flowers. But in Coriolanus, Lear, Romeo and Juliet, Hamlet, Othello, &c., the effect arises from the subordination of all to one, either as the prominent person, or the principal object. Cymbeline is the only exception; and even that has its advantages in preparing the audience for the chaos of time, place, and costume, by throwing the date back into a fabulous king's reign.

But as of more importance, so more striking, is the judgment displayed by our truly dramatic poet, as well as poet of the drama, in the management of his first scenes. With the single exception of Cymbeline, they either place before us at one glance both the past and the future in some effect, which implies the continuance and full agency of its cause, as in the feuds and party-spirit of the servants of the two houses in the first scene of Romeo and Juliet; or in the degrading passion for shows and public spectacles, and the overwhelming attachment for the newest successful war-chief in the Roman people, already become a populace, contrasted with the jealousy of the nobles in Julius Cæsar;—or they at once commence the action so as to excite a curiosity for the explanation in the following scenes, as in the storm of wind and waves, and the boatswain in the Tempest, instead of anticipating our curiosity, as in most other first scenes, and in too many other first acts;—or they act, by contrast of diction suited to the characters, at once to heighten the effect, and yet to give a naturalness to the language and rhythm of the principal personages, either as that of Prospero and Miranda by the appropriate lowness of the style, or as in King John, by the equally appropriate stateliness of official harangues or narratives, so that the after blank verse seems to belong to the rank and quality of the speakers, and not to the poet;— or they strike at once the key-note, and give the predominant spirit of the play, as in the Twelfth Night and in Macbeth;—or finally, the first scene comprises all these advantages at once, as in Hamlet.

Compare the easy language of common life, in which this drama commences, with the direful music and wild wayward rhythm and abrupt lyrics of the opening of Macbeth. The tone is quite familiar;—there is no poetic description of night, no elaborate information conveyed by one speaker to another of what both had immediately before their senses— (such as the first distich in Addison's Cato, which is a translation into poetry of "Past four o'clock and a dark morning!");—and yet nothing bordering on the comic on the one hand, nor any striving of the intellect on the other. It is precisely the language of sensation among men who feared no charge of effeminacy for feeling what they had no want of resolution to bear. Yet the armour, the dead silence, the watchfulness that first interrupts it, the welcome relief of the guard, the cold, the broken expressions of compelled attention to bodily feelings still under control—all excellently accord with, and prepare for, the after gradual rise into tragedy;—but, above all, into a tragedy, the interest of which is as eminently ad et apud intra, as that of Macbeth is directly ad extra.

In all the best attested stories of ghosts and visions, as in that of Brutus, of Archbishop Cranmer, that of Benvenuto Cellini recorded by himself, and the vision of Galileo communicated by him to his favourite pupil Torricelli, the ghost-seers were in a state of cold or chilling damp from without, and of anxiety inwardly. It has been with all of them as with Francisco on his guard,—alone, in the depth and silence of the night; "'twas bitter cold, and they were sick at heart, and not a mouse stirring." The attention to minute sounds,—naturally associated with the recollection of minute objects, and the more familiar and trifling, the more impressive from the unusualness of their producing any impression at all—gives a philosophic pertinency to this last image; but it has likewise its dramatic use and purpose. For its commonness in ordinary conversation tends to produce the sense of reality, and at once hides the poet, and yet approximates the reader or spectator to that state in which the highest poetry will appear, and in its component parts, though not in the whole composition, really is, the language of nature. If I should not speak it, I feel that I should be thinking it;—the voice only is the poet's,—the words are my own. That Shakespeare meant to put an effect in the actor's power in the very first words—"Who's there?"—is evident from the impatience expressed by the startled Francisco in the words that follow—"Nay, answer me: stand and unfold yourself." A brave man is never so peremptory, as when he fears that he is afraid. Observe the gradual transition from the silence and the still recent habit of listening in Francisco's—"I think I hear them"—to the more cheerful call out, which a good actor would observe, in the—"Stand ho! Who is there?" Bernardo's inquiry after Horatio, and the repetition of his name and in his own presence indicate a respect or an eagerness that implies him as one of the persons who are in the foreground; and the scepticism attributed to him,—

"Horatio says, 'tis but our fantasy;
And will not let belief take hold of him,"—
prepares us for Hamlet's after eulogy on him as one whose blood and judgment were happily commingled. The actor should also be careful to distinguish the expectation and gladness of Bernardo's "Welcome, Horatio!" from the mere courtesy of his "Welcome, good Marcellus!"

Now observe the admirable indefiniteness of the first opening out of the occasion of all this anxiety. The preparation informative of the audience is just as much as was precisely necessary, and no more;—it begins with the uncertainty appertaining to a question:—

"Mar. What, has this thing appear'd again to-night?"—
Even the word "again" has its credibilising effect. Then Horatio, the representative of the ignorance of the audience, not himself, but by Marcellus to Bernardo, anticipates the common solution—"'tis but our fantasy!" upon which Marcellus rises into—

"This dreaded sight, twice seen of us"—
which immediately afterwards becomes "this apparition," and that, too, an intelligent spirit—that is, to be spoken to! Then comes the confirmation of Horatio's disbelief;—

"Tush! tush! 'twill not appear!"—
and the silence, with which the scene opened, is again restored in the shivering feeling of Horatio sitting down, at such a time, and with the two eye-witnesses, to hear a story of a ghost, and that, too, of a ghost which had appeared twice before at the very same hour. In the deep feeling which Bernardo has of the solemn nature of what he is about to relate, he makes an effort to master his own imaginative terrors by an elevation of style,—itself a continuation of the effort,—and by turning off from the apparition, as from something

which would force him too deeply into himself, to the outward objects, the realities of nature, which had accompanied it:—

"Ber. Last night of all,
When yon same star, that's westward from the pole
Had made his course to illume that part of heaven
Where now it burns, Marcellus and myself,
The bell then beating one."

This passage seems to contradict the critical law that what is told, makes a faint impression compared with what is beholden; for it does indeed convey to the mind more than the eye can see; whilst the interruption of the narrative at the very moment when we are most intensely listening for the sequel, and have our thoughts diverted from the dreaded sight in expectation of the desired, yet almost dreaded, tale—this gives all the suddenness and surprise of the original appearance:—

"Mar. Peace, break thee off; look, where it comes again!"

Note the judgment displayed in having the two persons present, who, as having seen the Ghost before, are naturally eager in confirming their former opinions,—whilst the sceptic is silent, and after having been twice addressed by his friends, answers with two hasty syllables—"Most like,"—and a confession of horror:—

"It harrows me with fear and wonder."

O heaven! words are wasted on those who feel, and to those who do not feel the exquisite judgment of Shakespeare in this scene, what can be said? Hume himself could not but have had faith in this Ghost dramatically, let his anti-ghostism have been as strong as Sampson against other ghosts less powerfully raised.

Act i. sc. 1.—

"Mar. Good now, sit down, and tell me, he that knows,
Why this same strict and most observant watch," &c.

How delightfully natural is the transition, to the retrospective narrative! And observe, upon the Ghost's reappearance, how much Horatio's courage is increased by having translated the late individual spectator into general thought and past experience,—and the sympathy of Marcellus and Bernardo with his patriotic surmises in daring to strike at the Ghost; whilst in a moment, upon its vanishing, the former solemn awe-stricken feeling returns upon them:—

"We do it wrong, being so majestical,
To offer it the show of violence."
Ib. Horatio's speech:—

... "I have heard,
The cock, that is the trumpet to the morn,
Doth with his lofty and shrill-sounding throat
Awake the god of day," &c.

No Addison could be more careful to be poetical in diction than Shakespeare in providing the grounds and sources of its propriety. But how to elevate a thing almost mean by its familiarity, young poets may learn in this treatment of the cock-crow.

Ib. Horatio's speech:—

... "And, by my advice,
Let us impart what we have seen to-night
Unto young Hamlet; for, upon my life,
The spirit, dumb to us, will speak to him."

Note the inobtrusive and yet fully adequate mode of introducing the main character, "young Hamlet," upon whom it transferred all the interest excited for the acts and concerns of the king his father.

Ib. sc. 2. The audience are now relieved by a change of scene to the royal court, in order that Hamlet may not have to take up the leavings of exhaustion. In the king's speech, observe the set and pedantically antithetic form of the sentences when touching that which galled the heels of conscience,—the strain of undignified rhetoric,—and yet in what follows concerning the public weal, a certain appropriate majesty. Indeed was he not a royal brother?—

Ib. King's speech:—

"And now, Laertes, what's the news with you?" &c.

Thus with great art Shakespeare introduces a most important, but still subordinate character first, Laertes, who is yet thus graciously treated in consequence of the assistance given to the election of the late king's brother instead of his son by Polonius.

Ib.—

"Ham. A little more than kin, and less than kind.
King. How is it that the clouds still hang on you?
Ham. Not so, my lord, I am too much i' the sun."

Hamlet opens his mouth with a playing on words, the complete absence of which throughout characterises Macbeth. This playing on words may be attributed to many causes or motives, as either to an exuberant activity of mind, as in the higher comedy of Shakespeare generally;—or to an imitation of it as a mere fashion, as if it were said—"Is not this better than groaning?"—or to a contemptuous exultation in minds vulgarised and overset by their success, as in the poetic instance of Milton's Devils in the battle;—or it is the language of resentment, as is familiar to every one who has witnessed the quarrels of the lower orders, where there is invariably a profusion of punning invective, whence, perhaps, nicknames have in a considerable degree sprung up;—or it is the language of suppressed passion, and especially of a hardly smothered personal dislike. The first and last of these combine in Hamlet's case; and I have little doubt that Farmer is right in supposing the equivocation carried on in the expression "too much i' the sun," or son.

Ib.—

"Ham. Ay, madam, it is common."

Here observe Hamlet's delicacy to his mother, and how the suppression prepares him for the overflow in the next speech, in which his character is more developed by bringing forward his aversion to externals, and which betrays his habit of brooding over the world within him, coupled with a prodigality of beautiful words, which are the half embodyings of thought, and are more than thought, and have an outness, a reality sui generis, and yet retain their correspondence and shadowy affinity to the images and movements within. Note also Hamlet's silence to the long speech of the king which follows, and his respectful, but general, answer to his mother.

Ib. Hamlet's first soliloquy:—

"O, that this too too solid flesh would melt,
Thaw, and resolve itself into a dew!" &c.
This tædium vitæ is a common oppression on minds cast in the Hamlet mould, and is caused by disproportionate mental exertion, which necessitates exhaustion of bodily feeling. Where there is a just coincidence of external and internal action, pleasure is always the result; but where the former is deficient, and the mind's appetency of the ideal is unchecked, realities will seem cold and unmoving. In such cases, passion combines itself with the indefinite alone. In this mood of his mind the relation of the appearance of his father's spirit in arms is made all at once to Hamlet:—it is—Horatio's speech in particular—a perfect model of the true style of dramatic narrative;—the purest poetry, and yet in the most natural language, equally remote from the ink-horn and the plough.

Ib. sc. 3. This scene must be regarded as one of Shakespeare's lyric movements in the play, and the skill with which it is interwoven with the dramatic parts is peculiarly an excellence of our poet. You experience the sensation of a pause without the sense of a stop. You will observe in Ophelia's short and general answer to the long speech of Laertes the natural carelessness of innocence, which cannot think such a code of cautions and prudences necessary to its own preservation.

Ib. Speech of Polonius (in Stockdale's edition):—

"Or (not to crack the wind of the poor phrase),
Wronging it thus, you'll tender me a fool."
I suspect this "wronging" is here used much in the same sense as "wringing" or "wrenching," and that the parenthesis should be extended to "thus."

Ib. Speech of Polonius:—

... "How prodigal the soul
Lends the tongue vows:—these blazes, daughter," &c.

A spondee has, I doubt not, dropped out of the text. Either insert "Go to" after "vows";—

"Lends the tongue vows: Go to, these blazes, daughter"—
or read—

"Lends the tongue vows:—These blazes, daughter, mark you"—
Shakespeare never introduces a catalectic line without intending an equivalent to the foot omitted in the pauses, or the dwelling emphasis, or the diffused retardation. I do not, however, deny that a good actor might, by employing the last mentioned means—namely, the retardation, or solemn knowing drawl—supply the missing spondee with good effect. But I do not believe that in this or any other of the foregoing speeches of Polonius, Shakespeare meant to bring out the senility or weakness of that personage's mind. In the great ever-recurring dangers and duties of life, where to distinguish the fit objects for the application of the maxims collected by the experience of a long life, requires no fineness of tact, as in the admonitions to his son and daughter, Polonius is uniformly made respectable. But if an actor were even capable of catching these shades in the character, the pit and the gallery would be malcontent at their exhibition. It is to Hamlet that Polonius is, and is meant to be, contemptible, because in inwardness and uncontrollable activity of movement, Hamlet's mind is the logical contrary to that of Polonius; and besides, as I have observed

before, Hamlet dislikes the man as false to his true allegiance in the matter of the succession to the crown.

Ib. sc. 4. The unimportant conversation with which this scene opens is a proof of Shakespeare's minute knowledge of human nature. It is a well established fact, that on the brink of any serious enterprise, or event of moment, men almost invariably endeavour to elude the pressure of their own thoughts by turning aside to trivial objects and familiar circumstances: thus this dialogue on the platform begins with remarks on the coldness of the air, and inquiries, obliquely connected, indeed, with the expected hour of the visitation, but thrown out in a seeming vacuity of topics, as to the striking of the clock and so forth. The same desire to escape from the impending thought is carried on in Hamlet's account of, and moralizing on, the Danish custom of wassailing: he runs off from the particular to the universal, and, in his repugnance to personal and individual concerns, escapes, as it were, from himself in generalisations, and smothers the impatience and uneasy feelings of the moment in abstract reasoning. Besides this, another purpose is answered;—for by thus entangling the attention of the audience in the nice distinctions and parenthetical sentences of this speech of Hamlet's, Shakespeare takes them completely by surprise on the appearance of the Ghost, which comes upon them in all the suddenness of its visionary character. Indeed, no modern writer would have dared, like Shakespeare, to have preceded this last visitation by two distinct appearances,—or could have contrived that the third should rise upon the former two in impressiveness and solemnity of interest.

But in addition to all the other excellences of Hamlet's speech concerning the wassail-music—so finely revealing the predominant idealism, the ratiocinative meditativeness, of his character—it has the advantage of giving nature and probability to the impassioned continuity of the speech instantly directed to the Ghost. The momentum had been given to his mental activity; the full current of the thoughts and words had set in, and the very forgetfulness, in the fervour of his argumentation, of the purpose for which he was there, aided in preventing the appearance from benumbing the mind. Consequently, it acted as a new impulse,—a sudden stroke which increased the velocity of the body already in motion, whilst it altered the direction. The co-presence of Horatio, Marcellus, and Bernardo is most judiciously contrived; for it renders the courage of Hamlet, and his impetuous eloquence, perfectly intelligible. The knowledge,—the unthought of consciousness,—the sensation of human auditors—of flesh and blood sympathists—acts as a support and a stimulation a tergo, while the front of the mind, the whole consciousness of the speaker, is filled, yea, absorbed, by the apparition. Add too, that the apparition itself has, by its previous appearances, been brought nearer to a thing of this world. This accrescence of objectivity in a Ghost that yet retains all its ghostly attributes and fearful subjectivity, is truly wonderful.

Ib. sc. 5. Hamlet's speech:—

"O all you host of heaven! O earth! What else?
And shall I couple hell?"
I remember nothing equal to this burst, unless it be the first speech of Prometheus in the Greek drama, after the exit of Vulcan and the two Afrites. But Shakespeare alone could have produced the vow of Hamlet to make his memory a blank of all maxims and generalised truths, that "observation had copied there,"—followed immediately by the speaker noting down the generalised fact,—

"That one may smile, and smile, and be a villain!"
Ib.—

"Mar. Hillo, ho, ho, my lord!
Ham. Hillo, ho, ho, boy! come bird, come," &c.

This part of the scene, after Hamlet's interview with the Ghost, has been charged with an improbable eccentricity. But the truth is, that after the mind has been stretched beyond its usual pitch and tone, it must either sink into exhaustion and inanity, or seek relief by change. It is thus well known, that persons conversant in deeds of cruelty contrive to escape from conscience by connecting something of the ludicrous with them, and by inventing grotesque terms, and a certain technical phraseology, to disguise the horror of their practices. Indeed, paradoxical as it may appear, the terrible by a law of the human mind always touches on the verge of the ludicrous. Both arise from the perception of something out of the common order of things—something, in fact, out of its place; and if from this we can abstract danger, the uncommonness will alone remain, and the sense of the ridiculous be excited. The close alliance of these opposites—they are not contraries—appears from the circumstance, that laughter is equally the expression of extreme anguish and horror as of joy: as there are tears of sorrow and tears of joy, so is there a laugh of terror and a laugh of merriment. These complex causes will naturally have produced in Hamlet the disposition to escape from his own feelings of the overwhelming and supernatural by a wild transition to the ludicrous,—a sort of cunning bravado, bordering on the flights of delirium. For you may, perhaps, observe that Hamlet's wildness is but half false; he plays that subtle trick of pretending to act only when he is very near really being what he acts.

The subterraneous speeches of the Ghost are hardly defensible;—but I would call your attention to the characteristic difference between this Ghost, as a superstition connected with the most mysterious truths of revealed religion,—and Shakespeare's consequent reverence in his treatment of it,—and the foul earthly witcheries and wild language in Macbeth.

Act ii. sc. 1. Polonius and Reynaldo.

In all things dependent on, or rather made up of, fine address, the manner is no more or otherwise rememberable than the light notions, steps, and gestures of youth and health. But this is almost everything:—no wonder, therefore, if that which can be put down by rule in the memory should appear to us as mere poring, maudlin, cunning,—slyness blinking through the watery eye of superannuation. So in this admirable scene, Polonius, who is throughout the skeleton of his own former skill and statecraft, hunts the trail of policy at a dead scent, supplied by the weak fever-smell in his own nostrils.

Ib. sc. 2. Speech of Polonius:—

"My liege, and madam, to expostulate," &c.
Warburton's note.

"Then as to the jingles, and play on words, let us but look into the sermons of Dr. Donne (the wittiest man of that age), and we shall find them full of this vein."
I have, and that most carefully, read Dr. Donne's sermons, and find none of these jingles. The great art of an orator—to make whatever he talks of appear of importance—this, indeed, Donne has effected with consummate skill.

Ib.—

"Ham. Excellent well;
You are a fishmonger."

That is, you are sent to fish out this secret. This is Hamlet's own meaning.

Ib.—

"Ham. For if the sun breed maggots in a dead dog,
Being a god, kissing carrion."
These purposely obscure lines, I rather think, refer to some thought in Hamlet's mind, contrasting the lovely daughter with such a tedious old fool, her father, as he, Hamlet, represents Polonius to himself:—"Why, fool as he is, he is some degrees in rank above a dead dog's carcase; and if the sun, being a god that kisses carrion, can raise life out of a dead dog,—why may not good fortune, that favours fools, have raised a lovely girl out of this dead-alive old fool?" Warburton is often led astray, in his interpretations, by his attention to general positions without the due Shakespearian reference to what is probably passing in the mind of his speaker, characteristic, and expository of his particular character and present mood. The subsequent passage,—

"O Jephthah, judge of Israel! what a treasure hadst thou!"
is confirmatory of my view of these lines.

Ib.—

"Ham. You cannot, Sir, take from me any thing that I will
more willingly part withal; except my life, except my life, except
my life."
This repetition strikes me as most admirable.

Ib.—

"Ham. Then are our beggars, bodies; and our monarchs, and
out-stretched heroes, the beggars' shadows?"
I do not understand this; and Shakespeare seems to have intended the meaning not to be more than snatched at:—"By my fay, I cannot reason!"

Ib.—

"The rugged Pyrrhus—he whose sable arms," &c.
This admirable substitution of the epic for the dramatic, giving such a reality to the impassioned dramatic diction of Shakespeare's own dialogue, and authorised too, by the actual style of the tragedies before his time (Porrex and Ferrex, Titus Andronicus, &c.)—is well worthy of notice. The fancy, that a burlesque was intended, sinks below criticism: the lines, as epic narrative, are superb.

In the thoughts, and even in the separate parts of the diction, this description is highly poetical: in truth, taken by itself, that is its fault that it is too poetical!—the language of lyric vehemence and epic pomp, and not of the drama. But if Shakespeare had made the diction truly dramatic, where would have been the contrast between Hamlet and the play in Hamlet?

Ib.—

... "Had seen the mobled queen," &c.

A mob-cap is still a word in common use for a morning cap, which conceals the whole head of hair, and passes under the chin. It is nearly the same as the night-cap, that is, it is an imitation of it, so as to answer the purpose ("I am not drest for company"), and yet reconciling it with neatness and perfect purity.

Ib. Hamlet's soliloquy:—

"O, what a rogue and peasant slave am I!" &c.

This is Shakespeare's own attestation to the truth of the idea of Hamlet which I have before put forth.

Ib.—

"The spirit that I have seen,
May be a devil: and the devil hath power
To assume a pleasing shape; yea, and, perhaps
Out of my weakness, and my melancholy
(As he is very potent with such spirits),
Abuses me to damn me."
See Sir Thomas Brown:—

"I believe ... that those apparitions and ghosts of departed persons are not the wandering souls of men, but the unquiet walks of devils, prompting and suggesting us unto mischief, blood, and villany, instilling and stealing into our hearts, that the blessed spirits are not at rest in their graves, but wander solicitous of the affairs of the world."—Relig. Med. part. i. sect. 37.
Act iii. sc. 1. Hamlet's soliloquy:—

"To be, or not to be, that is the question," &c.
This speech is of absolutely universal interest,—and yet to which of all Shakespeare's characters could it have been appropriately given but to Hamlet? For Jaques it would have been too deep, and for Iago too habitual a communion with the heart; which in every man belongs, or ought to belong, to all mankind.

Ib.—

"The undiscover'd country, from whose bourn
No traveller returns."
Theobald's note in defence of the supposed contradiction of this in the apparition of the Ghost.

O miserable defender! If it be necessary to remove the apparent contradiction,—if it be not rather a great beauty,—surely, it were easy to say, that no traveller returns to this world, as to his home, or abiding-place.

Ib.—

"Ham. Ha, ha! are you honest?
Oph. My lord?
Ham. Are you fair?"

Here it is evident that the penetrating Hamlet perceives, from the strange and forced manner of Ophelia, that the sweet girl was not acting a part of her own, but was a decoy; and his after speeches are not so much directed to her as to the listeners and spies. Such a discovery in a mood so anxious and irritable accounts for a certain harshness in him;—and yet a wild up-working of love, sporting with opposites in a wilful self-tormenting strain of irony, is perceptible throughout. "I did love you once:"—"I lov'd you not:"—and particularly in his enumeration of the faults of the sex from which Ophelia is so free, that the mere freedom therefrom constitutes her character. Note Shakespeare's charm of composing the female character by the absence of characters, that is, marks and out-juttings.

Ib. Hamlet's speech:—

"I say, we will have no more marriages: those that are married already, all but one, shall live: the rest shall keep as they are."
Observe this dallying with the inward purpose, characteristic of one who had not brought his mind to the steady acting point. He would fain sting the uncle's mind;—but to stab his body!—The soliloquy of Ophelia, which follows, is the perfection of love—so exquisitely unselfish!

Ib. sc. 2. This dialogue of Hamlet with the players is one of the happiest instances of Shakespeare's power of diversifying the scene while he is carrying on the plot.

Ib.—

"Ham. My lord, you played once i' the university, you say?"
(To Polonius.)
To have kept Hamlet's love for Ophelia before the audience in any direct form, would have made a breach in the unity of the interest;—but yet to the thoughtful reader it is suggested by his spite to poor Polonius, whom he cannot let rest.

Ib. The style of the interlude here is distinguished from the real dialogue by rhyme, as in the first interview with the players by epic verse.

Ib.—

"Ros. My lord, you once did love me.
Ham. So I do still, by these pickers and stealers."
I never heard an actor give this word "so" its proper emphasis. Shakespeare's meaning is—"lov'd you? Hum!—so I do still," &c. There has been no change in my opinion:—I think as ill of you as I did. Else Hamlet tells an ignoble falsehood, and a useless one, as the last speech to Guildenstern—"Why look you now," &c.—proves.

Ib. Hamlet's soliloquy:—

"Now could I drink hot blood,
And do such business as the bitter day
Would quake to look on."
The utmost at which Hamlet arrives, is a disposition, a mood, to do something:—but what to do, is still left undecided, while every word he utters tends to betray his disguise. Yet observe how perfectly equal to any call of the moment is Hamlet, let it only not be for the future.

Ib. sc. 3. Speech of Polonius. Polonius's volunteer obtrusion of himself into this business, while it is appropriate to his character, still itching after former importance, removes all likelihood that Hamlet should suspect his presence, and prevents us from making his death injure Hamlet in our opinion.

Ib. The king's speech:—

"O, my offence is rank, it smells to heaven," &c.

This speech well marks the difference between crime and guilt of habit. The conscience here is still admitted to audience. Nay, even as an audible soliloquy, it is far less improbable than is supposed by such as have watched men only in the beaten road of their feelings. But the final—"all may be well!" is remarkable;—the degree of merit attributed by the self-flattering soul to its own struggle, though baffled, and to the indefinite half-promise, half-command, to persevere in religious duties. The solution is in the divine medium of the Christian doctrine of expiation:—not what you have done, but what you are, must determine.

Ib. Hamlet's speech:—

"Now might I do it, pat, now he is praying:
And now I'll do't:—And so he goes to heaven:
And so am I revenged? That would be scann'd," &c.
Dr. Johnson's mistaking of the marks of reluctance and procrastination for impetuous, horror-striking, fiendishness!—Of such importance is it to understand the germ of a character. But the interval taken by Hamlet's speech is truly awful! And then—

"My words fly up, my thoughts remain below:
Words, without thoughts, never to heaven go."
O what a lesson concerning the essential difference between wishing and willing, and the folly of all motive-mongering, while the individual self remains!

Ib. sc. 4.—

"Ham. A bloody deed;—almost as bad, good mother,
As kill a king, and marry with his brother.
Queen. As kill a king?"
I confess that Shakespeare has left the character of the Queen in an unpleasant perplexity. Was she, or was she not, conscious of the fratricide?

Act iv. sc. 2.—

"Ros. Take you me for a spunge, my lord?
Ham. Ay, Sir; that soaks up the King's countenance, his
rewards, his authorities," &c.
Hamlet's madness is made to consist in the free utterance of all the thoughts that had passed through his mind before;—in fact, in telling home-truths.

Act iv. sc. 5. Ophelia's singing. O, note the conjunction here of these two thoughts that had never subsisted in disjunction, the love for Hamlet, and her filial love, with the guileless floating on the surface of her pure imagination of the cautions so lately expressed, and the fears not too delicately avowed, by her father and brother, concerning the dangers to which her honour lay exposed. Thought, affliction, passion, murder itself—she turns to favour and prettiness. This play of association is instanced in the close:—

"My brother shall know of it, and I thank you for your good counsel."
Ib. Gentleman's speech:—

"And as the world were now but to begin
Antiquity forgot, custom not known,
The ratifiers and props of every word—
They cry," &c.
Fearful and self-suspicious as I always feel, when I seem to see an error of judgment in Shakespeare, yet I cannot reconcile the cool, and, as Warburton calls it, "rational and consequential," reflection in these lines with the anonymousness, or the alarm, of this Gentleman or Messenger, as he is called in other editions.

Ib. King's speech:—

"There's such divinity doth hedge a king,
That treason can but peep to what it would,
Acts little of his will."
Proof, as indeed all else is, that Shakespeare never intended us to see the King with Hamlet's eyes; though, I suspect, the managers have long done so.

Ib. Speech of Laertes:—

"To hell, allegiance! vows, to the blackest devil!"
"Laertes is a good character, but," &c.—Warburton.
Mercy on Warburton's notion of goodness! Please to refer to the seventh scene of this act;—

"I will do't;
And for that purpose I'll anoint my sword," &c.—
uttered by Laertes after the King's description of Hamlet;—

... "He being remiss,
Most generous, and free from all contriving,
Will not peruse the foils."
Yet I acknowledge that Shakespeare evidently wishes, as much as possible, to spare the character of Laertes,—to break the extreme turpitude of his consent to become an agent and accomplice of the King's treachery;—and to this end he re-introduces Ophelia at the close of this scene to afford a probable stimulus of passion in her brother.

Ib. sc. 6. Hamlet's capture by the pirates. This is almost the only play of Shakespeare, in which mere accidents, independent of all will, form an essential part of the plot;—but here how judiciously in keeping with the character of the over-meditative Hamlet, ever at last determined by accident or by a fit of passion!

Ib. sc. 7. Note how the King first awakens Laertes's vanity by praising the reporter, and then gratifies it by the report itself, and finally points it by—

... "Sir, this report of his
Did Hamlet so envenom with his envy!"

Ib. King's speech:—

"For goodness, growing to a pleurisy,
Dies in his own too much."
Theobald's note from Warburton, who conjectures "plethory."

I rather think that Shakespeare meant "pleurisy," but involved in it the thought of plethora, as supposing pleurisy to arise from too much blood; otherwise I cannot explain the following line—

"And then this should is like a spendthrift sigh,
That hurts by easing."
In a stitch in the side every one must have heaved a sigh that "hurt by easing."

Since writing the above I feel confirmed that "pleurisy" is the right word; for I find that in the old medical dictionaries the pleurisy is often called the "plethory."

Ib.—

"Queen. Your sister's drown'd, Laertes.
Laer. Drown'd! O, where?"
That Laertes might be excused in some degree for not cooling, the Act concludes with the affecting death of Ophelia,—who in the beginning lay like a little projection of land into a lake or stream, covered with spray-flowers, quietly reflected in the quiet waters, but at length is undermined or loosened, and becomes a faery isle, and after a brief vagrancy sinks almost without an eddy!

Act v. sc. 1. O, the rich contrast between the Clowns and Hamlet, as two extremes! You see in the former the mockery of logic, and a traditional wit valued, like truth, for its antiquity, and treasured up, like a tune, for use.

Ib. sc. 1 and 2. Shakespeare seems to mean all Hamlet's character to be brought together before his final disappearance from the scene;—his meditative excess in the grave-digging, his yielding to passion with Laertes, his love for Ophelia blazing out, his tendency to generalise on all occasions in the dialogue with Horatio, his fine gentlemanly manners with Osrick, and his and Shakespeare's own fondness for presentment:—

"But thou wouldst not think, how ill all's here about my heart: but it is no matter."

"Macbeth."

"Macbeth" stands in contrast throughout with Hamlet; in the manner of opening more especially. In the latter, there is a gradual ascent from the simplest forms of conversation to the language of impassioned intellect,—yet the intellect still remaining the seat of passion: in the former, the invocation is at once made to the imagination and the emotions connected therewith. Hence the movement throughout is the most rapid of all Shakespeare's plays; and hence also, with the exception of the disgusting passage of the Porter (Act ii. sc. 3), which I dare pledge myself to demonstrate to be an interpolation of the actors, there is not, to the best of my remembrance, a single pun or play on words in the whole drama. I have previously given an answer to the thousand times repeated charge against Shakespeare upon the subject of his punning, and I here merely mention the fact of the absence of any puns in Macbeth, as justifying a candid doubt, at least, whether even in these figures of speech and fanciful modifications of language, Shakespeare may not have followed rules and principles that merit and would stand the test of philosophic examination. And hence, also, there is an entire absence of comedy, nay, even of irony and philosophic contemplation in Macbeth,—the play being wholly and purely tragic. For the same cause, there are no reasonings of equivocal morality, which would have required a more leisurely state and a consequently greater activity of mind;—no sophistry of self-delusion,—except only that previously to the dreadful act, Macbeth mistranslates the recoilings and ominous whispers of conscience into prudential and selfish reasonings; and, after the deed done, the terrors of remorse into fear from external dangers,—like delirious men who run away from the phantoms of their own brains, or, raised by terror to rage, stab the real object that is within their reach:—whilst Lady Macbeth merely endeavours to reconcile his and her own sinkings of heart by anticipations of the worst, and an affected bravado in confronting them. In all the rest, Macbeth's language is the grave utterance of the very heart, conscience-sick, even to the last faintings of moral death. It is the same in all the other characters. The variety arises from rage, caused ever and anon by disruption of anxious thought, and the quick transition of fear into it.

In Hamlet and Macbeth the scene opens with superstition; but, in each it is not merely different, but opposite. In the first it is connected with the best and holiest feelings; in the second with the shadowy, turbulent, and unsanctified cravings of the individual will. Nor is the purpose the same; in the one the object is to excite, whilst in the other it is to mark a mind already excited. Superstition, of one sort or another, is natural to victorious generals; the instances are too notorious to need mentioning. There is so much of chance in warfare, and such vast events are connected with the acts of a single individual,—the representative, in truth, of the efforts of myriads, and yet to the public, and doubtless to his own feelings, the aggregate of all,—that the proper temperament for generating or receiving superstitious impressions is naturally produced. Hope, the master element of a commanding genius, meeting with an active and combining intellect, and an imagination of just that degree of vividness which disquiets and impels the soul to try to realise its images, greatly increases the creative power of the mind; and hence the images become a satisfying world of themselves, as is the case in every poet and original philosopher:—but hope fully gratified, and yet the elementary basis of the passion remaining, becomes fear; and, indeed, the general, who must often feel, even though he may hide it from his own consciousness, how large a share chance had in his successes, may very naturally be irresolute in a new scene, where he knows that all will depend on his own act and election.

The Weird Sisters are as true a creation of Shakespeare's, as his Ariel and Caliban,—fates, furies, and materialising witches being the elements. They are wholly different from any representation of witches in the contemporary writers, and yet presented a sufficient external resemblance to the creatures of vulgar prejudice to act immediately on the audience. Their character consists in the imaginative disconnected from the good; they are the shadowy obscure and fearfully anomalous of physical nature, the lawless of human nature,—elemental avengers without sex or kin:—

"Fair is foul, and foul is fair;
Hover through the fog and filthy air."
How much it were to be wished in playing Macbeth, that an attempt should be made to introduce the flexile character-mask of the ancient pantomime;—that Flaxman would

contribute his genius to the embodying and making sensuously perceptible that of Shakespeare!

The style and rhythm of the Captain's speeches in the second scene should be illustrated by reference to the interlude in Hamlet, in which the epic is substituted for the tragic, in order to make the latter be felt as the real-life diction. In Macbeth the poet's object was to raise the mind at once to the high tragic tone, that the audience might be ready for the precipitate consummation of guilt in the early part of the play. The true reason for the first appearance of the Witches is to strike the key-note of the character of the whole drama, as is proved by their re-appearance in the third scene, after such an order of the king's as establishes their supernatural power of information. I say information,—for so it only is as to Glamis and Cawdor; the "king hereafter" was still contingent,—still in Macbeth's moral will; although, if he should yield to the temptation, and thus forfeit his free agency, the link of cause and effect more physico would then commence. I need not say, that the general idea is all that can be required from the poet,—not a scholastic logical consistency in all the parts so as to meet metaphysical objectors. But O! how truly Shakespearian is the opening of Macbeth's character given in the unpossessedness of Banquo's mind, wholly present to the present object,—an unsullied, unscarified mirror! And how strictly true to nature it is that Banquo, and not Macbeth himself, directs our notice to the effect produced on Macbeth's mind, rendered temptible by previous dalliance of the fancy with ambitious thoughts:—

"Good Sir, why do you start; and seem to fear
Things that do sound so fair?"
And then, again, still unintroitive, addresses the Witches:—

... "I' the name of truth,
Are ye fantastical, or that indeed
Which outwardly ye show?"
Banquo's questions are those of natural curiosity,—such as a girl would put after hearing a gipsy tell her schoolfellow's fortune;—all perfectly general, or rather, planless. But Macbeth, lost in thought, raises himself to speech only by the Witches being about to depart:—

"Stay, you imperfect speakers, tell me more:"—
and all that follows is reasoning on a problem already discussed in his mind,—on a hope which he welcomes, and the doubts concerning the attainment of which he wishes to have cleared up. Compare his eagerness,—the keen eye with which he has pursued the Witches' evanishing—

"Speak, I charge you!"
with the easily satisfied mind of the self-uninterested Banquo:—

"The air hath bubbles, as the water has,
And these are of them:—Whither are they vanish'd?"
and then Macbeth's earnest reply,—

"Into the air; and what seem'd corporal, melted
As breath into the wind.—Would they had stay'd!"
Is it too minute to notice the appropriateness of the simile "as breath," &c., in a cold climate?

Still again Banquo goes on wondering like any common spectator,—

"Were such things here as we do speak about?"
whilst Macbeth persists in recurring to the self-concerning:—

"Your children shall be kings.
Ban. You shall be king.
Macb. And thane of Cawdor too: went it not so?"
So surely is the guilt in its germ anterior to the supposed cause, and immediate temptation! Before he can cool, the confirmation of the tempting half of the prophecy arrives, and the concatenating tendency of the imagination is fostered by the sudden coincidence:—

"Glamis, and thane of Cawdor:
The greatest is behind."
Oppose this to Banquo's simple surprise:—

"What, can the devil speak true?"
Ib. Banquo's speech:—

"That, trusted home,
Might yet enkindle you unto the crown,
Besides the thane of Cawdor."
I doubt whether "enkindle" has not another sense than that of "stimulating;" I mean of "kind" and "kin," as when rabbits are said to "kindle." However, Macbeth no longer hears anything ab extra:—

"Two truths are told,
As happy prologues to the swelling act
Of the imperial theme."
Then in the necessity of recollecting himself,—

"I thank you, gentlemen."
Then he relapses into himself again, and every word of his soliloquy shows the early birth-date of his guilt. He is all-powerful without strength; he wishes the end, but is irresolute as to the means; conscience distinctly warns him, and he lulls it imperfectly:—

"If chance will have me king, why, chance may crown me
Without my stir."
Lost in the prospective of his guilt, he turns round alarmed lest others may suspect what is passing in his own mind, and instantly vents the lie of ambition:—

"My dull brain was wrought
With things forgotten;"—
and immediately after pours forth the promising courtesies of a usurper in intention:—

... "Kind gentlemen, your pains
Are register'd where every day I turn
The leaf to read them."
Ib. Macbeth's speech:—

... "Present fears
Are less than horrible imaginings."
Warburton's note, and substitution of "feats" for "fears."

Mercy on this most wilful ingenuity of blundering, which, nevertheless, was the very Warburton of Warburton—his inmost being! "Fears," here, are present fear-striking objects, *terribilia adstantia*.

Ib. sc. 4. O! the affecting beauty of the death of Cawdor, and the presentimental speech of the king:—

"There's no art
To find the mind's construction in the face:
He was a gentleman on whom I built
An absolute trust."
Interrupted by—

"O worthiest cousin!"
on the entrance of the deeper traitor for whom Cawdor had made way! And here in contrast with Duncan's "plenteous joys," Macbeth has nothing but the common-places of loyalty, in which he hides himself with "our duties." Note the exceeding effort of Macbeth's addresses to the king, his reasoning on his allegiance, and then especially when a new difficulty, the designation of a successor, suggests a new crime. This, however, seems the first distinct notion, as to the plan of realising his wishes; and here, therefore, with great propriety, Macbeth's cowardice of his own conscience discloses itself. I always think there is something especially Shakespearian in Duncan's speeches throughout this scene, such pourings forth, such abandonments, compared with the language of vulgar dramatists, whose characters seem to have made their speeches as the actors learn them.

Ib: Duncan's speech:—

... "Sons, kinsmen, thanes,
And you whose places are the nearest, know,
We will establish our estate upon
Our eldest Malcolm, whom we name hereafter
The Prince of Cumberland: which honour must
Not unaccompanied, invest him only;
But signs of nobleness, like stars, shall shine
On all deservers."
It is a fancy;—but I can never read this and the following speeches of Macbeth, without involuntarily thinking of the Miltonic Messiah and Satan.

Ib. sc. 5. Macbeth is described by Lady Macbeth so as at the same time to reveal her own character. Could he have every thing he wanted, he would rather have it innocently;—ignorant, as alas! how many of us are, that he who wishes a temporal end for itself, does in truth will the means; and hence the danger of indulging fancies.

Lady Macbeth, like all in Shakespeare, is a class individualised:—of high rank, left much alone, and feeding herself with day-dreams of ambition, she mistakes the courage of fantasy for the power of bearing the consequences of the realities of guilt. His is the mock fortitude of a mind deluded by ambition; she shames her husband with a superhuman audacity of fancy which she cannot support, but sinks in the season of remorse, and dies in suicidal agony. Her speech:—

... "Come, you spirits
That tend on mortal thoughts, unsex me here," &c.—

is that of one who had habitually familiarised her imagination to dreadful conceptions, and was trying to do so still more. Her invocations and requisitions are all the false efforts of a mind accustomed only hitherto to the shadows of the imagination, vivid enough to throw the every-day substances of life into shadow, but never as yet brought into direct contact with their own correspondent realities. She evinces no womanly life, no wifely joy, at the return of her husband, no pleased terror at the thought of his past dangers, whilst Macbeth bursts forth naturally—

"My dearest love"—
and shrinks from the boldness with which she presents his own thoughts to him. With consummate art she at first uses as incentives the very circumstances, Duncan's coming to their house, &c., which Macbeth's conscience would most probably have adduced to her as motives of abhorrence or repulsion. Yet Macbeth is not prepared:—

"We will speak further."
Ib. sc. 6. The lyrical movement with which this scene opens, and the free and unengaged mind of Banquo, loving nature, and rewarded in the love itself, form a highly dramatic contrast with the laboured rhythm and hypocritical over-much of Lady Macbeth's welcome, in which you cannot detect a ray of personal feeling, but all is thrown upon the "dignities," the general duty.

Ib. sc. 7. Macbeth's speech:—

"We will proceed no further in this business:
He hath honour'd me of late; and I have bought
Golden opinions from all sorts of people,
Which would be worn now in their newest gloss,
Not cast aside so soon."
Note the inward pangs and warnings of conscience interpreted into prudential reasonings.

Act ii. sc. 1. Banquo's speech:—

"A heavy summons lies like lead upon me,
And yet I would not sleep. Merciful powers!
Restrain in me the cursed thoughts, that nature
Gives way to in repose."
The disturbance of an innocent soul by painful suspicions of another's guilty intentions and wishes, and fear of the cursed thoughts of sensual nature.

Ib. sc. 2. Now that the deed is done or doing—now that the first reality commences, Lady Macbeth shrinks. The most simple sound strikes terror, the most natural consequences are horrible, whilst previously every thing, however awful, appeared a mere trifle; conscience, which before had been hidden to Macbeth in selfish and prudential fears, now rushes in upon him in her own veritable person:—

"Methought I heard a voice cry—Sleep no more!
I could not say Amen,
When they did say, God bless us!"
And see the novelty given to the most familiar images by a new state of feeling.

Ib. sc. 3. This low soliloquy of the Porter and his few speeches afterwards, I believe to have been written for the mob by some other hand, perhaps with Shakespeare's consent; and that finding it take, he with the remaining ink of a pen otherwise employed, just interpolated the words—

"I'll devil-porter it no further: I had thought to have let in some of all professions, that go the primrose way to the everlasting bonfire."
Of the rest not one syllable has the ever-present being of Shakespeare.

Act iii. sc. 1. Compare Macbeth's mode of working on the murderers in this place with Schiller's mistaken scene between Butler, Devereux, and Macdonald in Wallenstein.—(Part II. act iv. sc. 2.) The comic was wholly out of season. Shakespeare never introduces it, but when it may react on the tragedy by harmonious contrast.

Ib. sc. 2. Macbeth's speech:—

"But let the frame of things disjoint, both the worlds suffer,
Ere we will eat our meal in fear, and sleep
In the affliction of these terrible dreams
That shake us nightly."
Ever and ever mistaking the anguish of conscience for fears of selfishness, and thus as a punishment of that selfishness, plunging still deeper in guilt and ruin.

Ib. Macbeth's speech:—

"Be innocent of the knowledge, dearest chuck,
Till thou applaud the deed."
This is Macbeth's sympathy with his own feelings, and his mistaking his wife's opposite state.

Ib. sc. 4.—

"Macb. It will have blood; they say, blood will have blood:
Stones have been known to move, and trees to speak;
Augurs, and understood relations, have
By magot-pies, and choughs, and rooks, brought forth
The secret'st man of blood."

The deed is done; but Macbeth receives no comfort, no additional security. He has by guilt torn himself live-asunder from nature, and is, therefore, himself in a preternatural state: no wonder, then, that he is inclined to superstition, and faith in the unknown of signs and tokens, and super-human agencies.

Act iv. sc. 1.—

"Len. 'Tis two or three, my lord, that bring you word
Macduff is fled to England.
Macb. Fled to England!"
The acme of the avenging conscience.

Ib. sc. 2. This scene, dreadful as it is, is still a relief, because a variety, because domestic, and therefore soothing, as associated with the only real pleasures of life. The conversation between Lady Macduff and her child heightens the pathos, and is preparatory for the deep tragedy of their assassination. Shakespeare's fondness for children is everywhere shown;—

in Prince Arthur, in King John; in the sweet scene in the Winter's Tale between Hermione and her son; nay, even in honest Evans's examination of Mrs. Page's schoolboy. To the objection that Shakespeare wounds the moral sense by the unsubdued, undisguised description of the most hateful atrocity—that he tears the feelings without mercy, and even outrages the eye itself with scenes of insupportable horror—I, omitting Titus Andronicus, as not genuine, and excepting the scene of Gloster's blinding in Lear, answer boldly in the name of Shakespeare, not guilty.

Ib. sc. 3. Malcolm's speech:—

... "Better Macbeth,
Than such an one to reign."

The moral is—the dreadful effects even on the best minds of the soul-sickening sense of insecurity.

Ib. How admirably Macduff's grief is in harmony with the whole play! It rends, not dissolves, the heart. "The tune of it goes manly." Thus is Shakespeare always master of himself and of his subject,—a genuine Proteus:—we see all things in him, as images in a calm lake, most distinct, most accurate,—only more splendid, more glorified. This is correctness in the only philosophical sense. But he requires your sympathy and your submission; you must have that recipiency of moral impression without which the purposes and ends of the drama would be frustrated, and the absence of which demonstrates an utter want of all imagination, a deadness to that necessary pleasure of being innocently—shall I say, deluded?—or rather, drawn away from ourselves to the music of noblest thought in harmonious sounds. Happy he, who not only in the public theatre, but in the labours of a profession, and round the light of his own hearth, still carries a heart so pleasure-fraught!

Alas for Macbeth! now all is inward with him; he has no more prudential prospective reasonings. His wife, the only being who could have had any seat in his affections, dies; he puts on despondency, the final heart-armour of the wretched, and would fain think every thing shadowy and unsubstantial, as indeed all things are to those who cannot regard them as symbols of goodness:—

"Out, out, brief candle!
Life's but a walking shadow; a poor player,
That struts and frets his hour upon the stage,
And then is heard no more; it is a tale
Told by an idiot, full of sound and fury,
Signifying nothing."

"Winter's Tale."

Although, on the whole, this play is exquisitely respondent to its title, and even in the fault I am about to mention, still a winter's tale; yet it seems a mere indolence of the great bard not to have provided in the oracular response (Act ii. sc. 2.) some ground for Hermione's seeming death and fifteen years' voluntary concealment. This might have been easily effected by some obscure sentence of the oracle, as for example:—

" 'Nor shall he ever recover an heir, if he have a wife before that recovery.' "

The idea of this delightful drama is a genuine jealousy of disposition, and it should be immediately followed by the perusal of Othello, which is the direct contrast of it in every particular. For jealousy is a vice of the mind, a culpable tendency of the temper, having certain well-known and well-defined effects and concomitants, all of which are visible in Leontes, and, I boldly say, not one of which marks its presence in Othello;—such as, first, an excitability by the most inadequate causes, and an eagerness to snatch at proofs; secondly, a grossness of conception, and a disposition to degrade the object of the passion by sensual fancies and images; thirdly, a sense of shame of his own feelings exhibited in a solitary moodiness of humour, and yet from the violence of the passion forced to utter itself, and therefore catching occasions to ease the mind by ambiguities, equivoques. by talking to those who cannot, and who are known not to be able to, understand what is said to them,—in short, by soliloquy in the form of dialogue, and hence a confused, broken, and fragmentary, manner; fourthly, a dread of vulgar ridicule, as distinct from a high sense of honour, or a mistaken sense of duty; and lastly, and immediately, consequent on this, a spirit of selfish vindictiveness.

Act i. sc. 1, 2.—

Observe the easy style of chitchat between Camillo and Archidamus as contrasted with the elevated diction on the introduction of the kings and Hermione in the second scene: and how admirably Polixenes' obstinate refusal to Leontes to stay,—

"There is no tongue that moves; none, none i' the world
So soon as yours, could win me;"—
prepares for the effect produced by his afterwards yielding to Hermione;—which is, nevertheless, perfectly natural from mere courtesy of sex, and the exhaustion of the will by former efforts of denial, and well calculated to set in nascent action the jealousy of Leontes. This, when once excited, is unconsciously increased by Hermione,—

... "Yet, good deed, Leontes,
I love thee not a jar o' the clock behind
What lady she her lord;"—
accompanied, as a good actress ought to represent it, by an expression and recoil of apprehension that she had gone too far.

"At my request, he would not:"—
The first working of the jealous fit;—

"Too hot, too hot:"—

The morbid tendency of Leontes to lay hold of the merest trifles, and his grossness immediately afterwards,—

"Paddling palms and pinching fingers;"—
followed by his strange loss of self-control in his dialogue with the little boy.

Act iii. sc. 2. Paulina's speech:—

"That thou betray'dst Polixenes, 'twas nothing;
That did but show thee, of a fool, inconstant,
And damnable ingrateful."
Theobald reads "soul."

I think the original word is Shakespeare's. 1. My ear feels it to be Shakespearian; 2. The involved grammar is Shakespearian—"show thee, being a fool naturally, to have improved thy folly by inconstancy;" 3. The alteration is most flat, and un-Shakespearian. As to the grossness of the abuse—she calls him "gross and foolish" a few lines below.

Act iv. sc. 3. Speech of Autolycus:—

"For the life to come, I sleep out the thought of it."
Fine as this is, and delicately characteristic of one who had lived and been reared in the best society, and had been precipitated from it by dice and drabbing; yet still it strikes against my feelings as a note out of tune, and as not coalescing with that pastoral tint which gives such a charm to this act. It is too Macbeth-like in the "snapper up of unconsidered trifles."

Ib. sc. 4. Perdita's speech:—

"From Dis's waggon! daffodils."
An epithet is wanted here, not merely or chiefly for the metre, but for the balance, for the æsthetic logic. Perhaps "golden" was the word which would set off the "violets dim."

Ib.—

... "Pale primroses
That die unmarried."
Milton's—

"And the rathe primrose that forsaken dies."
Ib. Perdita's speech:—

"Even here undone:
I was not much afraid; for once or twice
I was about to speak, and tell him plainly,
The self-same sun, that shines upon his court,
Hides not his visage from our cottage, but
Looks on alike. Will't please you, Sir, be gone!
(To Florizel.)
I told you, what would come of this. Beseech you,
Of your own state take care: this dream of mine,
Being now awake, I'll queen it no inch farther,
But milk my ewes, and weep."
O how more than exquisite is this whole speech! And that profound nature of noble pride and grief venting themselves in a momentary peevishness of resentment toward Florizel:—

... "Will't please you, Sir, be gone?"
Ib. Speech of Autolycus:—

"Let me have no lying; it becomes none but tradesmen, and they often give us soldiers the lie; but we pay them for it with stamped coin, not stabbing steel;—therefore they do not give us the lie."
As we pay them, they, therefore, do not give it us.

"Othello."

Act i. sc. 1.—

Admirable is the preparation, so truly and peculiarly Shakespearian, in the introduction of Roderigo, as the dupe on whom Iago shall first exercise his art, and in so doing display his own character. Roderigo, without any fixed principle, but not without the moral notions and sympathies with honour, which his rank and connections had hung upon him, is already well fitted and predisposed for the purpose; for very want of character and strength of passion, like wind loudest in an empty house, constitute his character. The first three lines happily state the nature and foundation of the friendship between him and Iago,—the purse,—as also the contrast of Roderigo's intemperance of mind with Iago's coolness,—the coolness of a preconceiving experimenter. The mere language of protestation,—

"If ever I did dream of such a matter, abhor me,"—
which, falling in with the associative link, determines Roderigo's continuation of complaint,—

"Thou told'st me, thou didst hold him in thy hate,"—
elicits at length a true feeling of Iago's mind, the dread of contempt habitual to those who encourage in themselves, and have their keenest pleasure in, the expression of contempt for others. Observe Iago's high self-opinion, and the moral, that a wicked man will employ real feelings, as well as assume those most alien from his own, as instruments of his purposes:—

"And, by the faith of man,
I know my price, I am worth no worse a place."
I think Tyrwhitt's reading of "life" for "wife"—

"A fellow almost damn'd in a fair wife"—
the true one, as fitting to Iago's contempt for whatever did not display power, and that intellectual power. In what follows, let the reader feel how by and through the glass of two passions, disappointed vanity and envy, the very vices of which he is complaining, are made to act upon him as if they were so many excellences, and the more appropriately, because cunning is always admired and wished for by minds conscious of inward weakness;—but they act only by half, like music on an inattentive auditor, swelling the thoughts which prevent him from listening to it.

Ib.—

"Rod. What a full fortune does the thick-lips owe,
If he can carry 't thus."
Roderigo turns off to Othello; and here comes one, if not the only, seeming justification of our blackamoor or negro Othello. Even if we supposed this an uninterrupted tradition of the theatre, and that Shakespeare himself, from want of scenes, and the experience that nothing could be made too marked for the senses of his audience, had practically sanctioned it,—would this prove aught concerning his own intention as a poet for all ages? Can we imagine him so utterly ignorant as to make a barbarous negro plead royal birth,—at a time, too, when negroes were not known except as slaves? As for Iago's language to Brabantio, it implies merely that Othello was a Moor,—that is, black. Though I think the rivalry of Roderigo sufficient to account for his wilful confusion of Moor and Negro,—yet, even if compelled to give this up, I should think it only adapted for the acting of the day, and should complain of an enormity built on a single word, in direct contradiction to Iago's

"Barbary horse." Besides, if we could in good earnest believe Shakespeare ignorant of the distinction, still why should we adopt one disagreeable possibility instead of a ten times greater and more pleasing probability? It is a common error to mistake the epithets applied by the dramatis personæ to each other, as truly descriptive of what the audience ought to see or know. No doubt Desdemona saw Othello's visage in his mind; yet, as we are constituted, and most surely as an English audience was disposed in the beginning of the seventeenth century, it would be something monstrous to conceive this beautiful Venetian girl falling in love with a veritable negro. It would argue a disproportionateness, a want of balance, in Desdemona, which Shakespeare does not appear to have in the least contemplated.

Ib. Brabantio's speech:—

"This accident is not unlike my dream."
The old careful senator, being caught careless, transfers his caution to his dreaming power at least.

Ib. Iago's speech:—

... "For their souls,
Another of his fathom they have not,
To lead their business."

The forced praise of Othello, followed by the bitter hatred of him in this speech! And observe how Brabantio's dream prepares for his recurrence to the notion of philtres, and how both prepare for carrying on the plot of the arraignment of Othello on this ground.

Ib. sc. 2.—

"Oth. 'Tis better as it is."
How well these few words impress at the outset the truth of Othello's own character of himself at the end—"that he was not easily wrought!" His self-government contradistinguishes him throughout from Leontes.

Ib. Othello's speech:—

... "And my demerits
May speak, unbonneted."
The argument in Theobald's note, where "and bonneted" is suggested, goes on the assumption that Shakespeare could not use the same word differently in different places; whereas I should conclude, that as in the passage in Lear the word is employed in its direct meaning, so here it is used metaphorically; and this is confirmed by what has escaped the editors, that it is not "I," but "my demerits" that may speak unbonneted,—without the symbol of a petitioning inferior.

Ib. sc. 3. Othello's speech:—

"So please your grace, my ancient;
A man he is of honesty and trust:
To his conveyance I assign my wife."
Compare this with the behaviour of Leontes to his true friend Camillo.

Ib.—

"Bra. Look to her, Moor; if thou hast eyes to see;
She has deceived her father, and may thee.
Oth. My life upon her faith."

In real life, how do we look back to little speeches as presentimental of, or contrasted with, an affecting event! Even so, Shakespeare, as secure of being read over and over, of becoming a family friend, provides this passage for his readers, and leaves it to them.

Ib. Iago's speech:—

"Virtue? a fig! 'tis in ourselves, that we are thus, or thus," &c.
This speech comprises the passionless character of Iago. It is all will in intellect; and therefore he is here a bold partizan of a truth, but yet of a truth converted into a falsehood by the absence of all the necessary modifications caused by the frail nature of man. And then comes the last sentiment:—

"Our raging motions, our carnal stings, our unbitted lusts, whereof I take this, that you call—love, to be a sect or scion!"
Here is the true Iagoism of, alas! how many! Note Iago's pride of mastery in the repetition of "Go, make money!" to his anticipated dupe, even stronger than his love of lucre: and when Roderigo is completely won,—

"I am chang'd. I'll go sell all my land,"—
when the effect has been fully produced, the repetition of triumph:—

"Go to; farewell; put money enough in your purse!"
The remainder—Iago's soliloquy—the motive-hunting of a motiveless malignity—how awful it is! Yea, whilst he is still allowed to bear the divine image, it is too fiendish for his own steady view,—for the lonely gaze of a being next to devil, and only not quite devil,—and yet a character which Shakespeare has attempted and executed, without disgust and without scandal!

Dr. Johnson has remarked that little or nothing is wanting to render the Othello a regular tragedy, but to have opened the play with the arrival of Othello in Cyprus, and to have thrown the preceding act into the form of narration. Here then is the place to determine whether such a change would or would not be an improvement;—nay (to throw down the glove with a full challenge), whether the tragedy would or not by such an arrangement become more regular,—that is, more consonant with the rules dictated by universal reason, on the true common-sense of mankind, in its application to the particular case. For in all acts of judgment, it can never be too often recollected, and scarcely too often repeated, that rules are means to ends, and, consequently, that the end must be determined and understood before it can be known what the rules are or ought to be. Now, from a certain species of drama, proposing to itself the accomplishment of certain ends,—these partly arising from the idea of the species itself, but in part, likewise, forced upon the dramatist by accidental circumstances beyond his power to remove or control,—three rules have been abstracted;—in other words, the means most conducive to the attainment of the proposed ends have been generalised, and prescribed under the names of the three unities,—the unity of time, the unity of place, and the unity of action—which last would, perhaps, have been as appropriately, as well as more intelligibly, entitled the unity of interest. With this last the present question has no immediate concern: in fact, its conjunction with the former two is a mere delusion of words. It is not properly a rule, but in itself the great end not only of the drama, but of the epic poem, the lyric ode, of all poetry, down to the candle-flame cone of an epigram,—nay, of poesy in general, as the proper generic term inclusive of all the fine arts as its species. But of the unities of time and place, which alone are entitled to the name of rules, the history of their origin will be their best criterion. You might take the Greek chorus to a place, but you could not bring a place to them without as palpable an equivoque as bringing Birnam wood to Macbeth at Dunsinane. It was the same, though in a less degree, with regard to the unity of time:—the positive fact, not for a moment removed from the senses, the presence, I mean, of the same identical chorus, was a continued measure of time;—and although the imagination may supersede perception, yet it must be granted to be an imperfection—however easily tolerated—to place the two in broad contradiction to each other. In truth, it is a mere accident of terms; for the Trilogy of the Greek theatre was a drama in three acts, and notwithstanding this, what strange contrivances as to place there are in the Aristophanic Frogs. Besides, if the law of mere actual perception is once violated—as it repeatedly is, even in the Greek tragedies—why is it more difficult to imagine three hours to be three years than to be a whole day and night?

Act ii. sc. 1.—

Observe in how many ways Othello is made, first, our acquaintance, then our friend, then the object of our anxiety, before the deeper interest is to be approached!

Ib.—

"Mont. But, good lieutenant, is your general wived?
Cas. Most fortunately: he hath achieved a maid
That paragons description, and wild fame;
One that excels the quirks of blazoning pens,
And, in the essential vesture of creation,
Does tire the ingener."
Here is Cassio's warm-hearted, yet perfectly disengaged, praise of Desdemona, and sympathy with the "most fortunately" wived Othello;—and yet Cassio is an enthusiastic admirer, almost a worshipper, of Desdemona. Oh, that detestable code that excellence cannot be loved in any form that is female, but it must needs be selfish! Observe Othello's "honest" and Cassio's "bold" Iago, and Cassio's full guileless-hearted wishes for the safety and love-raptures of Othello and "the divine Desdemona." And also note the exquisite circumstance of Cassio's kissing Iago's wife, as if it ought to be impossible that the dullest auditor should not feel Cassio's religious love of Desdemona's purity. Iago's answers are the sneers which a proud bad intellect feels towards women, and expresses to a wife. Surely it ought to be considered a very exalted compliment to women, that all the sarcasms on them in Shakespeare are put in the mouths of villains.

Ib.—

"Des. I am not merry; but I do beguile," &c.
The struggle of courtesy in Desdemona to abstract her attention.

Ib.—

"(Iago aside). He takes her by the palm: Ay, well said, whisper; with as little a web as this, will I ensnare as great a fly as Cassio. Ay, smile upon her, do," &c.
The importance given to trifles, and made fertile by the villany of the observer.

Ib. Iago's dialogue with Roderigo.

This is the rehearsal on the dupe of the traitor's intentions on Othello.

Ib. Iago's soliloquy:—

"But partly led to diet my revenge,
For that I do suspect the lusty Moor
Hath leap'd into my seat."
This thought, originally by Iago's own confession a mere suspicion, is now ripening, and gnaws his base nature as his own "poisonous mineral" is about to gnaw the noble heart of his general.

Ib. sc. 3. Othello's speech:—

"I know, Iago,
Thy honesty and love doth mince this matter,
Making it light to Cassio."
Honesty and love! Ay, and who but the reader of the play could think otherwise?

Ib. Iago's soliloquy:—

"And what's he then that says—I play the villain?
When this advice is free I give, and honest,
Provable to thinking, and, indeed, the course
To win the Moor again."
He is not, you see, an absolute fiend; or, at least, he wishes to think himself not so.

Act iii. sc. 3.—

"Des. Before Æmilia here,
I give thee warrant of thy place."
The over-zeal of innocence in Desdemona.

Ib.—

"Enter Desdemona and Æmilia.
Oth. If she be false, O, then, heaven mocks itself!
I'll not believe't."
Divine! The effect of innocence and the better genius!

Act iv. sc. 3.—

"Æmil. Why, the wrong is but a wrong i' the world; and
having the world for your labour, 'tis a wrong in your own world,
and you might quickly make it right."

Warburton's note.

What any other man, who had learning enough, might have quoted as a playful and witty illustration of his remarks against the Calvinistic thesis, Warburton gravely attributes to Shakespeare as intentional; and this, too, in the mouth of a lady's woman!

Act v. last scene. Othello's speech:—

... "Of one, whose hand,
Like the base Indian, threw a pearl away
Richer than all his tribe," &c.
Theobald's note from Warburton.

Thus it is for no-poets to comment on the greatest of poets! To make Othello say that he, who had killed his wife, was like Herod who killed Mariamne!—O, how many beauties, in this one line, were impenetrable to the ever thought-swarming, but idealess, Warburton! Othello wishes to excuse himself on the score of ignorance, and yet not to excuse himself,—to excuse himself by accusing. This struggle of feeling is finely conveyed in the word "base," which is applied to the rude Indian, not in his own character, but as the momentary representative of Othello's. "Indian"—for I retain the old reading—means American, a savage in genere.

Finally, let me repeat that Othello does not kill Desdemona in jealousy, but in a conviction forced upon him by the almost superhuman art of Iago, such a conviction as any man would and must have entertained who had believed Iago's honesty as Othello did. We, the audience, know that Iago is a villain, from the beginning; but in considering the essence of the Shakespearian Othello, we must perseveringly place ourselves in his situation, and under his circumstances. Then we shall immediately feel the fundamental difference between the solemn agony of the noble Moor, and the wretched fishing jealousies of Leontes, and the morbid suspiciousness of Leonatus, who is, in other respects, a fine character. Othello had no life but in Desdemona:—the belief that she, his angel, had fallen from the heaven of her native innocence, wrought a civil war in his heart. She is his counterpart; and, like him, is almost sanctified in our eyes by her absolute unsuspiciousness, and holy entireness of love. As the curtain drops, which do we pity the most?

Extremum hunc———. There are three powers:—Wit, which discovers partial likeness hidden in general diversity; subtlety, which discovers the diversity concealed in general apparent sameness;—and profundity, which discovers an essential unity under all the semblances of difference.

Give to a subtle man fancy, and he is a wit; to a deep man imagination, and he is a philosopher. Add, again, pleasurable sensibility in the threefold form of sympathy with the interesting in morals, the impressive in form, and the harmonious in sound,—and you have the poet.

But combine all,—wit, subtlety, and fancy, with profundity, imagination, and moral and physical susceptibility of the pleasurable,—and let the object of action be man universal; and we shall have—O, rash prophecy! say, rather, we have—a Shakespeare!

Notes on Ben Jonson.

It would be amusing to collect out of our dramatists from Elizabeth to Charles I. proofs of the manners of the times. One striking symptom of general coarseness of manners, which may co-exist with great refinement of morals, as, alas! vice versa, is to be seen in the very frequent allusions to the olfactories with their most disgusting stimulants, and these, too, in the conversation of virtuous ladies. This would not appear so strange to one who had been on terms of familiarity with Sicilian and Italian women of rank: and bad as they may, too many of them, actually be, yet I doubt not that the extreme grossness of their language has impressed many an Englishman of the present era with far darker notions than the same language would have produced in the mind of one of Elizabeth's or James's courtiers. Those who have read Shakespeare only, complain of occasional grossness in his plays; but compare him with his contemporaries, and the inevitable conviction, is that of the exquisite purity of his imagination.

The observation I have prefixed to the Volpone is the key to the faint interest which these noble efforts of intellectual power excite, with the exception of the fragment of the Sad Shepherd; because in that piece only is there any character with whom you can morally sympathise. On the other hand, Measure for Measure is the only play of Shakespeare's in which there are not some one or more characters, generally many, whom you follow with affectionate feeling. For I confess that Isabella, of all Shakespeare's female characters, pleases me the least; and Measure for Measure is, indeed, the only one of his genuine works, which is painful to me.

Let me not conclude this remark, however, without a thankful acknowledgment to the manes of Ben Jonson, that the more I study his writings, I the more admire them; and the more my study of him resembles that of an ancient classic, in the minutiæ of his rhythm, metre, choice of words, forms of connection, and so forth, the more numerous have the points of my admiration become. I may add, too, that both the study and the admiration cannot but be disinterested, for to expect therefrom any advantage to the present drama would be ignorance. The latter is utterly heterogeneous from the drama of the Shakespearian age, with a diverse object and contrary principle. The one was to present a model by imitation of real life, taking from real life all that in it which it ought to be, and supplying the rest;—the other is to copy what is, and as it is,—at best a tolerable but most frequently a blundering, copy. In the former the difference was an essential element; in the latter an involuntary defect. We should think it strange, if a tale in dance were announced, and the actors did not dance at all;—and yet such is modern comedy.

Whalley's Preface.

"But Jonson was soon sensible, how inconsistent this medley of names and manners was in reason and nature; and with how little propriety it could ever have a place in a legitimate and just picture of real life."

But did Jonson reflect that the very essence of a play, the very language in which it is written, is a fiction to which all the parts must conform? Surely, Greek manners in English should be a still grosser improbability than a Greek name transferred to English manners. Ben's personæ are too often not characters, but derangements;—the hopeless patients of a mad-doctor rather,—exhibitions of folly betraying itself in spite of exciting reason and prudence. He not poetically, but painfully exaggerates every trait; that is, not by the drollery of the circumstance, but by the excess of the originating feeling.

"But to this we might reply, that far from being thought to build his characters upon abstract ideas, he was really accused of representing particular persons then existing; and that even those characters which appear to be the most exaggerated, are said to have had their respective archetypes in nature and life."

This degrades Jonson into a libeller, instead of justifying him as a dramatic poet. Non quod verum est, sed quod verisimile, is the dramatist's rule. At all events, the poet who chooses transitory manners, ought to content himself with transitory praise. If his object be reputation, he ought not to expect fame. The utmost he can look forwards to, is to be quoted by, and to enliven the writings of, an antiquarian. Pistol, Nym, and id genus omne, do not please us as characters, but are endured as fantastic creations, foils to the native wit of Falstaff.—I say wit emphatically; for this character so often extolled as the masterpiece of humour, neither contains, nor was meant to contain, any humour at all.

"Whalley's 'Life Of Jonson.'"

"It is to the honour of Jonson's judgment, that the greatest poet of our nation had the same opinion of Donne's genius and wit; and hath preserved part of him from perishing, by putting his thoughts and satire into modern verse."
Videlicet Pope!—

"He said further to Drummond, Shakespeare wanted art, and sometimes sense; for in one of his plays he brought in a number of men, saying they had suffered shipwreck in Bohemia, where is no sea near by a hundred miles."
I have often thought Shakespeare justified in this seeming anachronism. In Pagan times a single name of a German kingdom might well be supposed to comprise a hundred miles more than at present. The truth is, these notes of Drummond's are more disgraceful to himself than to Jonson. It would be easy to conjecture how grossly Jonson must have been misunderstood, and what he had said in jest, as of Hippocrates, interpreted in earnest. But this is characteristic of a Scotchman; he has no notion of a jest, unless you tell him—"This is a joke!"—and still less of that finer shade of feeling, the half-and-half, in which Englishmen naturally delight.

"Every Man Out Of His Humour."

Epilogue.—

"The throat of war be stopt within her land,
And turtle-footed peace dance fairie rings
About her court."
"Turtle-footed" is a pretty word, a very pretty word: pray, what does it mean? Doves, I presume, are not dancers; and the other sort of turtle, land or sea, green-fat or hawksbill, would, I should suppose, succeed better in slow minuets than in the brisk rondillo. In one sense, to be sure, pigeons and ring-doves could not dance but with éclat—a claw!

"Poetaster."

Introduction.—

"Light! I salute thee, but with wounded nerves,
Wishing thy golden splendour pitchy darkness."
There is no reason to suppose Satan's address to the sun in the Paradise Lost, more than a mere coincidence with these lines; but were it otherwise, it would be a fine instance what usurious interest a great genius pays in borrowing. It would not be difficult to give a detailed psychological proof from these constant outbursts of anxious self-assertion, that Jonson was not a genius, a creative power. Subtract that one thing, and you may safely accumulate on his name all other excellences of a capacious, vigorous, agile, and richly-stored intellect.

Act i. sc. 1.—

"Ovid. While slaves be false, fathers hard, and bawds be whorish."

The roughness noticed by Theobald and Whalley, may be cured by a simple transposition:—

"While fathers hard, slaves false, and bawds be whorish."

Act. iv. sc. 3—

"Crisp. O—oblatrant—furibund—fatuate—strenuous.
O—conscious."

It would form an interesting essay, or rather series of essays, in a periodical work, were all the attempts to ridicule new phrases brought together, the proportion observed of words ridiculed which have been adopted, and are now common, such as strenuous, conscious, &c., and a trial made how far any grounds can be detected, so that one might determine beforehand whether a word was invented under the conditions of assimilability to our language or not. Thus much is certain, that the ridiculers were as often wrong as right; and Shakespeare himself could not prevent the naturalisation of accommodation, remuneration, &c.; or Swift the gross abuse even of the word idea.

"Fall Of Sejanus."

Act i.—

"Arruntius. The name Tiberius,
I hope, will keep, howe'er he hath foregone
The dignity and power.
Silius. Sure, while he lives.
Arr. And dead, it comes to Drusus. Should he fail,
To the brave issue of Germanicus;
And they are three: too many (ha?) for him
To have a plot upon?
Sil. I do not know
The heart of his designs; but, sure, their face
Looks farther than the present.
Arr. By the gods,
If I could guess he had but such a thought,
My sword should cleave him down," &c.

The anachronic mixture in this Arruntius of the Roman republican, to whom Tiberius must have appeared as much a tyrant as Sejanus, with his James-and-Charles-the-First zeal for legitimacy of descent in this passage, is amusing. Of our great names Milton was, I think, the first who could properly be called a republican. My recollections of Buchanan's works are too faint to enable me to judge whether the historian is not a fair exception.

Act ii. Speech of Sejanus:—

"Adultery! it is the lightest ill
I will commit. A race of wicked acts
Shall flow out of my anger, and o'erspread

The world's wide face, which no posterity
Shall e'er approve, nor yet keep silent," &c.

The more we reflect and examine, examine and reflect, the more astonished shall we be at the immense superiority of Shakespeare over his contemporaries;—and yet what contemporaries!—giant minds indeed! Think of Jonson's erudition, and the force of learned authority in that age; and yet, in no genuine part of Shakespeare's works is there to be found such an absurd rant and ventriloquism as this, and too, too many other passages ferruminated by Jonson from Seneca's tragedies, and the writings of the later Romans. I call it ventriloquism, because Sejanus is a puppet, out of which the poet makes his own voice appear to come.

Act v. Scene of the sacrifice to Fortune.

This scene is unspeakably irrational. To believe, and yet to scoff at, a present miracle is little less than impossible. Sejanus should have been made to suspect priestcraft and a secret conspiracy against him.

"Volpone."

This admirable, indeed, but yet more wonderful than admirable, play is, from the fertility and vigour of invention, character, language, and sentiment, the strongest proof how impossible it is to keep up any pleasurable interest in a tale, in which there is no goodness of heart in any of the prominent characters. After the third act, this play becomes not a dead, but a painful, weight on the feelings. Zeluco is an instance of the same truth. Bonario and Celia should have been made in some way or other principals in the plot; which they might have been, and the objects of interest, without having been made characters. In novels, the person in whose fate you are most interested, is often the least marked character of the whole. If it were possible to lessen the paramountcy of Volpone himself, a most delightful comedy might be produced, by making Celia the ward or niece of Corvino, instead of his wife, and Bonario her lover.

"Apicæne."

This is to my feelings the most entertaining of old Ben's comedies, and, more than any other, would admit of being brought out anew, if under the management of a judicious and stage-understanding playwright; and an actor, who had studied Morose, might make his fortune.

Act i. sc. 1. Clerimont's speech:—

"He would have hang'd a pewterer's 'prentice once upon a Shrove
Tuesday's riot, for being of that trade, when the rest were quiet."
"The old copies read quit,—i.e., discharged from working, and gone to divert themselves."—Whalley's note.

It should be "quit" no doubt, but not meaning "discharged from working," &c.—but quit, that is, acquitted. The pewterer was at his holiday diversion as well as the other apprentices, and they as forward in the riot as he. But he alone was punished under pretext of the riot, but in fact for his trade.

Act ii. sc. 1.—

"Morose. Cannot I, yet, find out a more compendious method than by this trunk, to save my servants the labour of speech, and mine ears the discord of sounds?"
What does "trunk" mean here, and in the first scene of the first act? Is it a large ear-trumpet?—or rather a tube, such as passes from parlour to kitchen, instead of a bell?

Whalley's note at the end:—

"Some critics of the last age imagined the character of Morose to be wholly out of nature. But to vindicate our poet, Mr. Dryden tells us from tradition, and we may venture to take his word, that Jonson was really acquainted with a person of this whimsical turn of mind: and as humour is a personal quality, the poet is acquitted from the charge of exhibiting a monster, or an extravagant unnatural caricatura."
If Dryden had not made all additional proof superfluous by his own plays, this very vindication would evince that he had formed a false and vulgar conception of the nature and conditions of drama and dramatic personation. Ben Jonson would himself have rejected such a plea:—

"For he knew, poet never credit gain'd
By writing truths, but things, like truths, well feign'd."
By "truths" he means "facts." Caricatures are not less so because they are found existing in real life. Comedy demands characters, and leaves caricatures to farce. The safest and the truest defence of old Ben would be to call the Epicœne the best of farces. The defect in Morose, as in other of Jonson's dramatis personæ, lies in this;—that the accident is not a prominence growing out of, and nourished by, the character which still circulates in it; but that the character, such as it is, rises out of, or, rather, consists in, the accident. Shakespeare's comic personages have exquisitely characteristic features; however awry, disproportionate, and laughable they may be, still, like Bardolph's nose, they are features. But Jonson's are either a man with a huge wen, having a circulation of its own, and which we might conceive amputated, and the patient thereby losing all his character; or they are mere wens themselves instead of men,—wens personified, or with eyes, nose, and mouth cut out, mandrake-fashion.

Nota bene.—All the above, and much more, will have justly been said, if, and whenever, the drama of Jonson is brought into comparisons of rivalry with the Shakespearian. But this should not be. Let its inferiority to the Shakespearian be at once fairly owned,—but at the same time as the inferiority of an altogether different genius of the drama. On this ground, old Ben would still maintain his proud height. He, no less than Shakespeare stands on the summit of his hill, and looks round him like a master,—though his be Lattrig and Shakespeare's Skiddaw.

"The Alchemist."

Act i. sc. 2. Face's speech:—

"Will take his oath o' the Greek Xenophon,
If need be, in his pocket."
Another reading is "Testament."

Probably, the meaning is—that intending to give false evidence, he carried a Greek Xenophon to pass it off for a Greek Testament, and so avoid perjury—as the Irish do, by contriving to kiss their thumb-nails instead of the book.

Act ii. sc. 2. Mammon's speech:—

"I will have all my beds blown up; not stuft:
Down is too hard."

Thus the air-cushions, though perhaps only lately brought into use, were invented in idea in the seventeenth century!

"Catiline's Conspiracy."

A fondness for judging one work by comparison with others, perhaps altogether of a different class, argues a vulgar taste. Yet it is chiefly on this principle that the Catiline has been rated so low. Take it and Sejanus, as compositions of a particular kind, namely, as a mode of relating great historical events in the liveliest and most interesting manner, and I cannot help wishing that we had whole volumes of such plays. We might as rationally expect the excitement of the Vicar of Wakefield from Goldsmith's History of England, as that of Lear, Othello, &c., from the Sejanus or Catiline.

Act i. sc. 4.—

"Cat. Sirrah, what ail you?
(He spies one of his boys not answer.)
Pag. Nothing.
Best. Somewhat modest.
Cat. Slave, I will strike your soul out with my foot," &c.

This is either an unintelligible, or, in every sense, a most unnatural, passage,—improbable, if not impossible, at the moment of signing and swearing such a conspiracy, to the most libidinous satyr. The very presence of the boys is an outrage to probability. I suspect that these lines down to the words "throat opens," should be removed back so as to follow the words "on this part of the house," in the speech of Catiline soon after the entry of the conspirators. A total erasure, however, would be the best, or, rather, the only possible, amendment.

Act ii. sc. 2. Sempronia's speech:—

..."He is but a new fellow,
An inmate here in Rome, as Catiline calls him."
A "lodger" would have been a happier imitation of the inquilinus of Sallust.

Act iv. sc. 6. Speech of Cethegus:—

"Can these or such be any aids to us," &c.
What a strange notion Ben must have formed of a determined, remorseless, all-daring, foolhardiness, to have represented it in such a mouthing Tamburlane, and bombastic tonguebully as this Cethegus of his!

"Bartholomew Fair."

Induction. Scrivener's speech:—

"If there be never a servant-monster in the Fair, who can help it
he says, nor a nest of antiques?"

The best excuse that can be made for Jonson, and in a somewhat less degree for Beaumont and Fletcher, in respect of these base and silly sneers at Shakespeare is, that his plays were present to men's minds chiefly as acted. They had not a neat edition of them, as we have, so as, by comparing the one with the other, to form a just notion of the mighty mind that produced the whole. At all events, and in every point of view, Jonson stands far higher in a moral light than Beaumont and Fletcher. He was a fair contemporary, and in his way, and as far as Shakespeare is concerned, an original. But Beaumont and Fletcher were always imitators of, and often borrowers from him, and yet sneer at him with a spite far more malignant than Jonson, who, besides, has made noble compensation by his praises.

Act ii. sc. 3.—

"Just. I mean a child of the horn-thumb, a babe of booty, boy, a
cut purse."

Does not this confirm, what the passage itself cannot but suggest, the propriety of substituting "booty" for "beauty" in Falstaff's speech, Henry IV. part i. act i. sc. 2. "Let not us, &c.?"

It is not often that old Ben condescends to imitate a modern author; but Master Dan. Knockhum Jordan, and his vapours are manifest reflexes of Nym and Pistol.

Ib. sc. 5.—

"Quarl. She'll make excellent geer for the coachmakers here in
Smithfield, to anoint wheels and axletrees with."

Good! but yet it falls short of the speech of a Mr. Johnes, M.P., in the Common Council, on the invasion intended by Buonaparte:—"Houses plundered—then burnt;—sons conscribed—wives and daughters ravished," &c., &c.—"But as for you, you luxurious Aldermen! with your fat will he grease the wheels of his triumphant chariot!"

Ib. sc. 6.—

"Cok. Avoid in your satin doublet, Numps."

This reminds me of Shakespeare's "Aroint thee, witch!" I find in several books of that age the words aloigne and eloigne—that is,—"keep your distance!" or "off with you!" Perhaps "aroint" was a corruption of "aloigne" by the vulgar. The common etymology from ronger to gnaw seems unsatisfactory.

Act iii. sc. 4.—

"Quarl. How now, Numps! almost tired in your protectorship?
overparted, overparted?"

An odd sort of propheticality in this Numps and old Noll!

Ib. sc. 6. Knockhum's speech:—

"He eats with his eyes, as well as his teeth."

A good motto for the Parson in Hogarth's Election Dinner,—who shows how easily he might be reconciled to the Church of Rome, for he worships what he eats.

Act v. sc. 5.—

"Pup. Di. It is not profane.
Lan. It is not profane, he says.
Boy. It is profane.
Pup. It is not profane.
Boy. It is profane.
Pup. It is not profane.
Lan. Well said, confute him with Not, still."
An imitation of the quarrel between Bacchus and the Frogs in Aristophanes:—

"Χορός.
ἀλλὰ μὴν κεκραξόμεσθά γ',
ὁπόσον ἡ φάρυνξ ἂν ἡμῶν
χανδάνῃ δι' ἡμέρας,
βρεκεκεκὲξ, κοὰξ, κοὰξ.
Διόνυσος.
τούτῳ γὰρ οὐ νικήσετε.
Χορός.
οὐδὲ μὴν ἡμᾶς σὺ τάντως.
Διόνυσος.
οὐδὲ μὴν ὑμεῖς γε δή μ' οὐδέποτε."

"The Devil Is An Ass."

Act i. sc. 1.—

"Pug. Why any: Fraud,
Or Covetousness, or lady Vanity,
Or old Iniquity, I'll call him hither."
"The words in italics should probably be given to the master-devil, Satan."—Whalley's note. That is, against all probability, and with a (for Jonson) impossible violation of character. The words plainly belong to Pug, and mark at once his simpleness and his impatience.

Ib. sc. 4. Fitz-dottrel's soliloquy.

Compare this exquisite piece of sense, satire, and sound philosophy in 1616 with Sir M. Hale's speech from the bench in a trial of a witch many years afterwards.

Act ii. sc. 1. Meercraft's speech:—

"Sir, money's a whore, a bawd, a drudge."
I doubt not that "money" was the first word of the line, and has dropped out:—

"Money! Sir, money's a," &c.

"The Staple Of News."

Act iv. sc. 3. Pecunia's speech:—

"No, he would ha' done,

That lay not in his power: he had the use
Of your bodies, Band and Wax, and sometimes Statute's."
Read (1815)—

... "he had the use of
Your bodies," &c.
Now, however, I doubt the legitimacy of my transposition of the "of" from the beginning of this latter line to the end of the one preceding;—for though it facilitates the metre and reading of the latter line, and is frequent in Massinger, this disjunction of the preposition from its case seems to have been disallowed by Jonson. Perhaps the better reading is—

"O' your bodies," &c.—
the two syllables being slurred into one, or rather snatched, or sucked, up into the emphasised "your." In all points of view, therefore, Ben's judgment is just; for in this way, the line cannot be read, as metre, without that strong and quick emphasis on "your" which the sense requires;—and had not the sense required an emphasis on "your," the tmesis of the sign of its cases "of," "to," &c., would destroy almost all boundary between the dramatic verse and prose in comedy:—a lesson not to be rash in conjectural amendments.—1818.

Ib. sc. 4.—

"P. jun. I love all men of virtue, frommy Princess."
"Frommy," fromme—pious, dutiful, &c.

Act v. sc. 4. Penny-boy, sen., and Porter.

I dare not, will not, think that honest Ben had Lear in his mind in this mock mad scene.

"The New Inn."

Act i. sc. 1. Host's speech:—

"A heavy purse, and then two turtles, makes."
"Makes," frequent in old books, and even now used in some counties for mates, or pairs.

Ib. sc. 3. Host's speech:—

..."And for a leap
Of the vaulting horse, to play the vaulting house."
Instead of reading with Whalley "ply" for "play," I would suggest "horse" for "house." The meaning would then be obvious and pertinent. The punlet, or pun-maggot, or pun intentional, "horse and house," is below Jonson. The jeu-de-mots just below—

..."Read a lecture
Upon Aquinas at St. Thomas à Waterings"—
had a learned smack in it to season its insipidity.

Ib. sc. 6. Lovel's speech:—

"Then shower'd his bounties on me, like the Hours,
That open-handed sit upon the clouds,
And press the liberality of heaven
Down to the laps of thankful men!"

Like many other similar passages in Jonson, this is εἶδος χαλεπὸν ἰδεῖν—a sight which it is difficult to make one's self see,—a picture my fancy cannot copy detached from the words.

Act ii. sc. 5. Though it was hard upon old Ben, yet Felton, it must be confessed, was in the right in considering the Fly, Tipto, Bat Burst, &c., of this play mere dotages. Such a scene as this was enough to damn a new play; and Nick Stuff is worse still,—most abominable stuff indeed!

Act iii. sc. 2. Lovel's speech:—

"So knowledge first begets benevolence,
Benevolence breeds friendship, friendship love."

Jonson has elsewhere proceeded thus far; but the part most difficult and delicate, yet, perhaps, not the least capable of being both morally and poetically treated, is the union itself, and what, even in this life, it can be.

Notes On Beaumont And Fletcher.

Seward's Preface. 1750.—

"The King and No King, too, is extremely spirited in all its characters; Arbaces holds up a mirror to all men of virtuous principles but violent passions. Hence he is, as it were, at once magnanimity and pride, patience and fury, gentleness and rigour, chastity and incest, and is one of the finest mixtures of virtues and vices that any poet has drawn," &c.

These are among the endless instances of the abject state to which psychology had sunk from the reign of Charles I. to the middle of the present reign of George III.; and even now it is but just awaking.

Ib. Seward's comparison of Julia's speech in the Two Gentlemen of Verona, act iv. last scene—

"Madam, 'twas Ariadne passioning," &c.
with Aspatia's speech in the Maid's Tragedy—

"I stand upon the sea-beach now," &c.—Act ii.—
and preference of the latter.

It is strange to take an incidental passage of one writer, intended only for a subordinate part, and compare it with the same thought in another writer, who had chosen it for a prominent and principal figure.

Ib. Seward's preference of Alphonso's poisoning in A Wife for a Month, act i. sc. 1, to the passage in King John, act v. sc. 7:—

"Poison'd, ill fare! dead, forsook, cast off!"
Mr. Seward! Mr. Seward! you may be, and I trust you are, an angel; but you were an ass.

Ib.—

"Every reader of taste will see how superior this is to the quotation from Shakespeare."
Of what taste?

Ib. Seward's classification of the plays.

Surely Monsieur Thomas, the Chances, Beggar's Bush, and the Pilgrim, should have been placed in the very first class! But the whole attempt ends in a woful failure.

Harris's Commendatory Poem On Fletcher.

"I'd have a state of wit convok'd, which hath
A power to take up on common faith:"—
This is an instance of that modifying of quantity by emphasis, without which our elder poets cannot be scanned. "Power," here, instead of being one long syllable—pow'r—must be sounded, not indeed as a spondee, nor yet as a trochee; but as - u u;—the first syllable is 1-1/4.

We can, indeed, never expect an authentic edition of our elder dramatic poets (for in those times a drama was a poem), until some man undertakes the work, who has studied the philosophy of metre. This has been found the main torch of sound restoration in the Greek dramatists by Bentley, Porson, and their followers;—how much more, then, in writers in our own language! It is true that quantity, an almost iron law with the Greek, is in English rather a subject for a peculiarly fine ear, than any law or even rule; but, then, instead of it, we have, first, accent; secondly, emphasis; and lastly, retardation, and acceleration of the times of syllables according to the meaning of the words, the passion that accompanies them, and even the character of the person that uses them. With due attention to these,— above all, to that, which requires the most attention and the finest taste, the character, Massinger, for example, might be reduced to a rich and yet regular metre. But then the regulæ must be first known; though I will venture to say, that he who does not find a line (not corrupted) of Massinger's flow to the time total of a trimeter catalectic iambic verse, has not read it aright. But by virtue of the last principle—the retardation of acceleration of time—we have the proceleusmatic foot u u u u, and the dispondæus - - - -, not to mention the choriambus, the ionics, pæons, and epitrites. Since Dryden, the metre of our poets leads to the sense; in our elder and more genuine bards, the sense, including the passion, leads to the metre. Read even Donne's satires as he meant them to be read, and as the sense and passion demand, and you will find in the lines a manly harmony.

Life Of Fletcher In Stockdale's Edition, 1811.

"In general their plots are more regular than Shakespeare's."
This is true, if true at all, only before a court of criticism, which judges one scheme by the laws of another and a diverse one. Shakespeare's plots have their own laws of regulæ, and according to these they are regular.

"Maid's Tragedy."

Act i. The metrical arrangement is most slovenly throughout.

"Strat. As well as masque can be," &c.—
and all that follows to "who is return'd"—is plainly blank verse, and falls easily into it.

Ib. Speech of Melantius:—

"These soft and silken wars are not for me:
The music must be shrill, and all confus'd,
That stirs my blood; and then I dance with arms."
What strange self-trumpeters and tongue-bullies all the brave soldiers of Beaumont and Fletcher are! Yet I am inclined to think it was the fashion of the age from the Soldier's speech in the Counter Scuffle; and deeper than the fashion B. and F. did not fashion.

Ib. Speech of Lysippus:—

"Yes, but this lady
Walks discontented, with her wat'ry eyes
Bent on the earth," &c.
Opulent as Shakespeare was, and of his opulence prodigal, he yet would not have put this exquisite piece of poetry in the mouth of a no-character, or as addressed to a Melantius. I wish that B. and F. had written poems instead of tragedies.

Ib.—

"Mel. I might run fiercely, not more hastily,
Upon my foe."
Read

"I mĭght rūn mŏre fiērcelȳ, not more hastily."

Ib. Speech of Calianax:—

"Office! I would I could put it off! I am sure I sweat quite through my office!"
The syllable off reminds the testy statesman of his robe, and he carries on the image.

Ib. Speech of Melantius:—

... "Would that blood,
That sea of blood, that I have lost in fight," &c.
All B. and F.'s generals are pugilists or cudgel-fighters, that boast of their bottom and of the claret they have shed.

Ib. The Masque;—Cinthia's speech:—

"But I will give a greater state and glory,
And raise to time a noble memory
Of what these lovers are."
I suspect that "nobler," pronounced as "nobiler" - u -, was the poet's word, and that the accent is to be placed on the penultimate of "memory." As to the passage—

"Yet, while our reign lasts, let us stretch our power," &c.—

removed from the text of Cinthia's speech, by these foolish editors as unworthy of B. and F.—the first eight lines are not worse, and the last couplet incomparably better, than the stanza retained.

Act ii. Amintor's speech:—

"Oh, thou hast nam'd a word, that wipes away
All thoughts revengeful! In that sacred name,
'The king,' there lies a terror."
It is worth noticing that of the three greatest tragedians, Massinger was a democrat, Beaumont and Fletcher the most servile jure divino royalists, and Shakespeare a philosopher;—if aught personal, an aristocrat.

"A King And No King."

Act iv. Speech of Tigranes:—

"She, that forgat the greatness of her grief
And miseries, that must follow such mad passions,
Endless and wild as women!" &c.
Seward's note and suggestion of "in."

It would be amusing to learn from some existing friend of Mr. Seward what he meant, or rather dreamed, in this note. It is certainly a difficult passage, of which there are two solutions;—one, that the writer was somewhat more injudicious than usual;—the other, that he was very, very much more profound and Shakespearian than usual. Seward's emendation, at all events, is right and obvious. Were it a passage of Shakespeare, I should not hesitate to interpret it as characteristic of Tigranes' state of mind, disliking the very virtues, and therefore half-consciously representing them as mere products of the violence of the sex in general in all their whims, and yet forced to admire, and to feel and to express gratitude for, the exertion in his own instance. The inconsistency of the passage would be the consistency of the author. But this is above Beaumont and Fletcher.

"The Scornful Lady."

Act ii. Sir Roger's speech:—

"Did I for this consume my quarters in meditations, vows, and woo'd her in heroical epistles? Did I expound the Owl, and undertake, with labour and expense, the recollection of those thousand pieces, consum'd in cellars and tobacco-shops, of that our honour'd Englishman, Nic. Broughton?" &c.
Strange, that neither Mr. Theobald nor Mr. Seward should have seen that this mock heroic speech is in full-mouthed blank verse! Had they seen this, they would have seen that "quarters" is a substitution of the players for "quires" or "squares," (that is) of paper:—

"Consume my quires in meditations, vows,
And woo'd her in heroical epistles."
They ought, likewise, to have seen that the abbreviated "Ni. Br." of the text was properly "Mi. Dr."—and that Michael Drayton, not Nicholas Broughton, is here ridiculed for his poem The Owl and his Heroical Epistles.

Ib. Speech of Younger Loveless:—

"Fill him some wine. Thou dost not see me mov'd," &c.
These Editors ought to have learnt, that scarce an instance occurs in B. and F. of a long speech not in metre. This is plain staring blank verse.

"The Custom Of The Country."

I cannot but think that in a country conquered by a nobler race than the natives, and in which the latter became villeins and bondsmen, this custom, lex merchetæ, may have been introduced for wise purposes,—as of improving the breed, lessening the antipathy of different races, and producing a new bond of relationship between the lord and the tenant, who, as the eldest born, would at least have a chance of being, and a probability of being thought, the lord's child. In the West Indies it cannot have these effects, because the mulatto is marked by nature different from the father, and because there is no bond, no law, no custom, but of mere debauchery.—1815.

Act i. sc. 1. Rutilio's speech:—

"Yet if you play not fair play," &c.
Evidently to be transposed, and read thus:—

"Yet if you play not fair, above-board too,
I'll tell you what—
I've a foolish engine here:—I say no more—
But if your Honour's guts are not enchanted."
Licentious as the comic metre of B. and F. is,—a far more lawless, and yet far less happy, imitation of the rhythm of animated talk in real life than Massinger's—still it is made worse than it really is by ignorance of the halves, thirds, and two-thirds of a line which B. and F. adopted from the Italian and Spanish dramatists. Thus, in Rutilio's speech:—

"Though I confess
Any man would desire to have her, and by any means," &c.
Correct the whole passage,—

"Though I confess
Any man would
Desire to have her, and by any means,
At any rate too, yet this common hangman
That hath whipt off a thousănd măids heads already—
That he should glean the harvest, sticks in my stomach!"
In all comic metres the gulping of short syllables, and the abbreviation of syllables ordinarily long by the rapid pronunciation of eagerness and vehemence, are not so much a license as a law,—a faithful copy of nature, and let them be read characteristically, the times will be found nearly equal. Thus, the three words marked above make a choriambus -- u u, or perhaps a pæon primus - u u u; a dactyl, by virtue of comic rapidity, being only equal to an iambus when distinctly pronounced. I have no doubt that all B. and F.'s works might be safely corrected by attention to this rule, and that the editor is entitled to transpositions of

all kinds, and to not a few omissions. For the rule of the metre once lost—what was to restrain the actors from interpolation?

"The Elder Brother."

Act i. sc. 2. Charles's speech:—

... "For what concerns tillage,
Who better can deliver it than Virgil
In his Georgicks? and to cure your herds,
His Bucolicks is a master-piece."
Fletcher was too good a scholar to fall into so gross a blunder, as Messrs. Sympson and Colman suppose. I read the passage thus:—

... "For what concerns tillage,
Who better can deliver it than Virgil,
In his Georgicks, or to cure your herds
(His Bucolicks are a master-piece); but when," &c.
Jealous of Virgil's honour, he is afraid lest, by referring to the Georgics alone, he might be understood as undervaluing the preceding work. "Not that I do not admire the Bucolics too, in their way.—But when," &c.

Act iii. sc. 3. Charles's speech:—

... "She has a face looks like a story;
The story of the heavens looks very like her."
Seward reads "glory;" and Theobald quotes from Philaster:—

"That reads the story of a woman's face."
I can make sense of this passage as little as Mr. Seward;—the passage from Philaster is nothing to the purpose. Instead of "a story," I have sometimes thought of proposing "Astræa."

Ib. Angellina's speech:—

... "You're old and dim, Sir,
And the shadow of the earth eclips'd your judgment."
Inappropriate to Angellina, but one of the finest lines in our language.

Act iv. sc. 3. Charles's speech:—

"And lets the serious part of life run by
As thin neglected sand, whiteness of name.
You must be mine," &c.
Seward's note, and reading:—

... "Whiteness of name,
You must be mine!"

Nonsense! "Whiteness of name" is in apposition to "the serious part of life," and means a deservedly pure reputation. The following line—"You must be mine!" means—"Though I do not enjoy you to-day, I shall hereafter, and without reproach."

"The Spanish Curate."

Act iv. sc. 7. Amaranta's speech:—

"And still I push'd him on, as he had been coming."
Perhaps the true word is "conning,"—that is, learning, or reading, and therefore inattentive.

"Wit Without Money."

Act i. Valentine's speech:—

"One without substance," &c.
The present text, and that proposed by Seward, are equally vile. I have endeavoured to make the lines sense, though the whole is, I suspect, incurable except by bold conjectural reformation. I would read thus:—

"One without substance of herself, that's woman;
Without the pleasure of her life, that's wanton;
Tho' she be young, forgetting it; tho' fair,
Making her glass the eyes of honest men,
Not her own admiration."
"That's wanton," or, "that is to say, wantonness."

Act ii. Valentine's speech:—

"Of half-a crown a week for pins and puppets."
"As there is a syllable wanting in the measure here."—Seward.
A syllable wanting! Had this Seward neither ears nor fingers? The line is a more than usually regular iambic hendecasyllable.

Ib.—

"With one man satisfied, with one rein guided;
With one faith, one content, one bed;
Aged, she makes the wife, preserves the fame and issue;
A widow is," &c.
Is "apaid"—contented—too obsolete for B. and F.? If not, we might read it thus:—

"Content with one faith, with one bed apaid,
She makes the wife, preserves the fame and issue;"—

Or, it may be,—

... "with one breed apaid"—
that is, satisfied with one set of children, in opposition to,—

"A widow is a Christmas-box," &c.

Colman's note on Seward's attempt to put this play into metre.

The editors, and their contemporaries in general, were ignorant of any but the regular iambic verse. A study of the Aristophanic and Plautine metres would have enabled them to reduce B. and F. throughout into metre, except where prose is really intended.

"The Humorous Lieutenant."

Act i. sc. 1. Second Ambassador's speech:—

... "When your angers,
Like so many brother billows, rose together,
And, curling up your foaming crests, defied," &c.
This worse than superfluous "like" is very like an interpolation of some matter of fact critic—all pus, prose atque venenum. The "your" in the next line, instead of "their," is likewise yours, Mr. Critic!

Act ii. sc. 1. Timon's speech:—

"Another of a new way will be look'd at."
"We must suspect the poets wrote, 'of a new day.' So immediately after,

... Time may
For all his wisdom, yet give us a day."
Seward's Note.

For this very reason I more than suspect the contrary.

Ib. sc. 3. Speech of Leucippe:—

"I'll put her into action for a wastcoat."
What we call a riding-habit,—some mannish dress.

"The Mad Lover."

Act iv. Masque of beasts:—

... "This goodly tree,
An usher that still grew before his lady,
Wither'd at root: this, for he could not woo,
A grumbling lawyer:" &c.
Here must have been omitted a line rhyming to "tree;" and the words of the next line have been transposed:—

... "This goodly tree,
Which leafless, and obscur'd with moss you see,
An usher this, that 'fore his lady grew,
Wither'd at root: this, for he could not woo," &c.

"The Loyal Subject."

It is well worthy of notice, and yet has not been, I believe, noticed hitherto, what a marked difference there exists in the dramatic writers of the Elizabetho-Jacobæan age—(Mercy on me! what a phrase for "the writers during the reigns of Elizabeth and James I.!")—in respect of their political opinions. Shakespeare, in this, as in all other things, himself and alone, gives the permanent politics of human nature, and the only predilection which appears, shows itself in his contempt of mobs and the populacy. Massinger is a decided Whig;—Beaumont and Fletcher high-flying, passive-obedience, Tories. The Spanish dramatists furnished them with this, as with many other ingredients. By the by, an accurate and familiar acquaintance with all the productions of the Spanish stage previously to 1620, is an indispensable qualification for an editor of B. and F.;—and with this qualification a most interesting and instructive edition might be given. This edition of Colman's (Stockdale, 1811) is below criticism.

In metre, B. and F. are inferior to Shakespeare, on the one hand, as expressing the poetic part of the drama, and to Massinger, on the other, in the art of reconciling metre with the natural rhythm of conversation,—in which, indeed, Massinger is unrivalled. Read him aright, and measure by time, not syllables, and no lines can be more legitimate,—none in which the substitution of equipollent feet, and the modifications by emphasis, are managed with such exquisite judgment. B. and F. are fond of the twelve syllable (not Alexandrine) line, as:—

"Too many fears 'tis thought too: and to nourish those."
This has often a good effect, and is one of the varieties most common in Shakespeare.

"Rule A Wife And Have A Wife."

Act iii. Old Woman's speech:—

... "I fear he will knock my
Brains out for lying."
Mr. Seward discards the words "for lying," because "most of the things spoke of Estifania are true, with only a little exaggeration, and because they destroy all appearance of measure."—Colman's note.

Mr. Seward had his brains out. The humour lies in Estifania's having ordered the Old Woman to tell these tales of her; for though an intriguer, she is not represented as other than chaste; and as to the metre, it is perfectly correct.

Ib.—

"Marg. As you love me, give way.
Leon. It shall be better, I will give none, madam," &c.
The meaning is:—"It shall be a better way, first;—as it is, I will not give it, or any that you in your present mood would wish."

"The Laws Of Candy."

Act i. Speech of Melitus:—

"Whose insolence and never yet match'd pride
Can by no character be well express'd,
But in her only name, the proud Erota."
Colman's note.

The poet intended no allusion to the word "Erota" itself; but says that her very name, "the proud Erota," became a character and adage;—as we say, a Quixote or a Brutus: so to say an "Erota," expressed female pride and insolence of beauty.

Ib. Speech of Antinous:—

"Of my peculiar honours, not deriv'd
From successary, but purchas'd with my blood."
The poet doubtless wrote "successry," which, though not adopted in our language, would be, on many occasions, as here, a much more significant phrase than ancestry.

"The Little French Lawyer."

Act i. sc. 1. Dinant's speech:—

"Are you become a patron too? 'Tis a new one,
No more on't," &c.
Seward reads:—

"Are you become a patron too? How long
Have you been conning this speech? 'Tis a new one," &c.
If conjectural emendation like this be allowed, we might venture to read:—

"Are you become a patron to a new tune?"
or,—

"Are you become a patron? 'Tis a new tune."
Ib.—

"Din. Thou wouldst not willingly
Live a protested coward, or be call'd one?
Cler. Words are but words.
Din. Nor wouldst thou take a blow?"
Seward's note.

O miserable! Dinant sees through Cleremont's gravity, and the actor is to explain it. "Words are but words," is the last struggle of affected morality.

"Valentinian."

Act i. sc. 3.—

It is a real trial of charity to read this scene with tolerable temper towards Fletcher. So very slavish—so reptile—are the feelings and sentiments represented as duties. And yet, remember, he was a bishop's son, and the duty to God was the supposed basis.

Personals, including body, house, home, and religion;—property, subordination, and inter-community;—these are the fundamentals of society. I mean here, religion negatively taken,—so that the person be not compelled to do or utter, in relation of the soul to God, what would be, in that person, a lie;—such as to force a man to go to church, or to swear that he believes what he does not believe. Religion, positively taken, may be a great and useful privilege, but cannot be a right,—were it for this only, that it cannot be pre-defined. The ground of this distinction between negative and positive religion, as a social right, is plain. No one of my fellow-citizens is encroached on by my not declaring to him what I believe respecting the super-sensual; but should every man be entitled to preach against the preacher, who could hear any preacher? Now, it is different in respect of loyalty. There we have positive rights, but not negative rights;—for every pretended negative would be in effect a positive;—as if a soldier had a right to keep to himself whether he would, or would not, fight. Now, no one of these fundamentals can be rightfully attacked, except when the guardian of it has abused it to subvert one or more of the rest. The reason is, that the guardian, as a fluent, is less than the permanent which he is to guard. He is the temporary and mutable mean, and derives his whole value from the end. In short, as robbery is not high treason, so neither is every unjust act of a king the converse. All must be attacked and endangered. Why? Because the king, as a to A, is a mean to A, or subordination, in a far higher sense than a proprietor, as b to A, is a mean to B, or property.

Act ii. sc. 2. Claudia's speech:—

"Chimney-pieces!" &c.
The whole of this speech seems corrupt; and if accurately printed,—that is, if the same in all the prior editions,—irremediable but by bold conjecture. "Till my tackle," should be, I think, "While," &c.

Act iii. sc. 1. B. and F. always write as if virtue or goodness were a sort of talisman, or strange something, that might be lost without the least fault on the part of the owner. In short, their chaste ladies value their chastity as a material thing,—not as an act or state of being; and this mere thing being imaginary, no wonder that all their women are represented with the minds of strumpets, except a few irrational humourists, far less capable of exciting our sympathy than a Hindoo who has had a basin of cow-broth thrown over him;—for this, though a debasing superstition, is still real, and we might pity the poor wretch, though we cannot help despising him. But B. and F.'s Lucinas are clumsy fictions. It is too plain that the authors had no one idea of chastity as a virtue, but only such a conception as a blind man might have of the power of seeing by handling an ox's eye. In The Queen of Corinth, indeed, they talk differently; but it is all talk, and nothing is real in it but the dread of losing a reputation. Hence the frightful contrast between their women (even those who are meant for virtuous) and Shakespeare's. So, for instance, The Maid in the Mill:—a woman must not merely have grown old in brothels, but have chuckled over every abomination committed in them with a rampant sympathy of imagination, to have had her fancy so drunk with the minutiæ of lechery as this icy chaste virgin evinces hers to have been.

It would be worth while to note how many of these plays are founded on rapes,—how many on incestuous passions, and how many on mere lunacies. Then their virtuous women are either crazy superstitions of a mere bodily negation of having been acted on, or strumpets in their imaginations and wishes, or, as in this Maid in the Mill, both at the same time. In the men, the love is merely lust in one direction,—exclusive preference of one object. The tyrant's speeches are mostly taken from the mouths of indignant denouncers of the tyrant's character, with the substitution of "I" for "he,"" and the omission of the prefatory "he acts as if he thought" so and so. The only feelings they can possibly excite are disgust at the Æciuses, if regarded as sane loyalists, or compassion if considered as Bedlamites. So much for their tragedies. But even their comedies are, most of them, disturbed by the fantasticalness, or gross caricature, of the persons or incidents. There are few characters that you can really like (even though you should have erased from your mind all the filth which bespatters the most likeable of them, as Piniero in The Island Princess for instance),—scarcely one whom you can love. How different this from Shakespeare, who makes one have a sort of sneaking affection even for his Barnardines;—whose very Iagos and Richards are awful, and, by the counteracting power of profound intellects, rendered fearful rather than hateful;—and even the exceptions, as Goneril and Regan, are proofs of superlative judgment and the finest moral tact, in being left utter monsters, nulla virtute redemptæ, and in being kept out of sight as much as possible,—they being, indeed, only means for the excitement and deepening of noblest emotions towards the Lear, Cordelia, &c. and employed with the severest economy! But even Shakespeare's grossness—that which is really so, independently of the increase in modern times of vicious associations with things indifferent (for there is a state of manners conceivable so pure, that the language of Hamlet at Ophelia's feet might be a harmless rallying, or playful teazing, of a shame that would exist in Paradise)—at the worst, how diverse in kind is it from Beaumont and Fletcher's! In Shakespeare it is the mere generalities of sex, mere words for the most part, seldom or never distinct images, all head-work, and fancy drolleries; there is no sensation supposed in the speaker. I need not proceed to contrast this with B. and F.

"Rollo."

This, perhaps, the most energetic of Fletcher's tragedies. He evidently aimed at a new Richard III. in Rollo;—but, as in all his other imitations of Shakespeare, he was not philosopher enough to bottom his original. Thus, in Rollo, he has produced a mere personification of outrageous wickedness, with no fundamental characteristic impulses to make either the tyrant's words or actions philosophically intelligible. Hence the most pathetic situations border on the horrible, and what he meant for the terrible, is either hateful, τὸ μισητὸν, or ludicrous. The scene of Baldwin's sentence in the third act is probably the grandest working of passion in all B. and F.'s dramas;—but the very magnificence of filial affection given to Edith, in this noble scene, renders the after scene (in imitation of one of the least Shakespearian of all Shakespeare's works, if it be his, the scene between Richard and Lady Anne) in which Edith is yielding to a few words and tears, not only unnatural, but disgusting. In Shakespeare, Lady Anne is described as a weak, vain, very woman throughout.

Act i. sc. 1.—

"Gis. He is indeed the perfect character
Of a good man, and so his actions speak him."
This character of Aubrey, and the whole spirit of this and several other plays of the same authors, are interesting as traits of the morals which it was fashionable to teach in the reigns of James I. and his successor, who died a martyr to them. Stage, pulpit, law, fashion,—all conspired to enslave the realm. Massinger's plays breathe the opposite spirit; Shakespeare's

the spirit of wisdom which is for all ages. By the by, the Spanish dramatists—Calderon, in particular,—had some influence in this respect, of romantic loyalty to the greatest monsters, as well as in the busy intrigues of B. and F.'s plays.

"The Wildgoose Chase."

Act ii. sc. 1. Belleur's speech:—

... "That wench, methinks,
If I were but well set on, for she is a fable,
If I were but hounded right, and one to teach me."
Sympson reads "affable," which Colman rejects, and says, "the next line seems to enforce" the reading in the text.

Pity, that the editor did not explain wherein the sense, "seemingly enforced by the next line," consists. May the true word be "a sable"—that is, a black fox, hunted for its precious fur? Or "at-able,"—as we now say,—"she is come-at-able?"

"A Wife For A Month."

Act iv. sc. 1. Alphonso's speech:—

"Betwixt the cold bear and the raging lion
Lies my safe way."
Seward's note and alteration to—

"'Twixt the cold bears, far from the raging lion"—
This Mr. Seward is a blockhead of the provoking species. In his itch for correction, he forgot the words—"lies my safe way!" The bear is the extreme pole, and thither he would travel over the space contained between it and "the raging lion."

"The Pilgrim."

Act iv. sc. 2.—

Alinda's interview with her father is lively, and happily hit off; but this scene with Roderigo is truly excellent. Altogether, indeed, this play holds the first place in B. and F.'s romantic entertainments, Lustspiele, which collectively are their happiest performances, and are only inferior to the romance of Shakespeare in the As You Like It, Twelfth Night, &c.

Ib.—

"Alin. To-day you shall wed Sorrow,
And Repentance will come to-morrow."
Read "Penitence," or else—

"Repentance, she will come to-morrow."

"The Queen Of Corinth."

Act ii. sc. 1.—

Merione's speech. Had the scene of this tragi-comedy been laid in Hindostan instead of Corinth, and the gods here addressed been the Vishnu and Co. of the Indian Pantheon, this rant would not have been much amiss.

In respect of style and versification, this play and the following of Bonduca may be taken as the best, and yet as characteristic, specimens of Beaumont and Fletcher's dramas. I particularly instance the first scene of the Bonduca. Take Shakespeare's Richard II., and having selected some one scene of about the same number of lines, and consisting mostly of long speeches, compare it with the first scene in Bonduca,—not for the idle purpose of finding out which is the better, but in order to see and understand the difference. The latter, that of B. and F., you will find a well-arranged bed of flowers, each having its separate root, and its position determined aforehand by the will of the gardener,—each fresh plant a fresh volition. In the former you see an Indian fig-tree, as described by Milton;—all is growth, evolution;—each line, each word almost, begets the following, and the will of the writer is an interfusion, a continuous agency, and not a series of separate acts. Shakespeare is the height, breadth, and depth of Genius: Beaumont and Fletcher the excellent mechanism, in juxta-position and succession, of talent.

"The Noble Gentleman."

Why have the dramatists of the times of Elizabeth, James I., and the first Charles become almost obsolete, with the exception of Shakespeare? Why do they no longer belong to the English, being once so popular? And why is Shakespeare an exception?—One thing, among fifty, necessary to the full solution is, that they all employed poetry and poetic diction on unpoetic subjects, both characters and situations, especially in their comedy. Now Shakespeare is all, all ideal,—of no time, and therefore for all times. Read, for instance, Marine's panegyric in the first scene of this play:—

... "Know
The eminent court, to them that can be wise,
And fasten on her blessings, is a sun," &c.

What can be more unnatural and inappropriate (not only is, but must be felt as such) than such poetry in the mouth of a silly dupe? In short, the scenes are mock dialogues, in which the poet solus plays the ventriloquist, but cannot keep down his own way of expressing himself. Heavy complaints have been made respecting the transposing of the old plays by Cibber; but it never occurred to these critics to ask, how it came that no one ever attempted to transpose a comedy of Shakespeare's.

"The Coronation."

Act i. Speech of Seleucus:—

"Altho' he be my enemy, should any
Of the gay flies that buz about the court,
Sit to catch trouts i' the summer, tell me so,
I durst," &c.
Colman's note.

Pshaw! "Sit" is either a misprint for "set," or the old and still provincial word for "set," as the participle passive of "seat" or "set." I have heard an old Somersetshire gardener say:— "Look, Sir! I set these plants here; those yonder I sit yesterday."

Act ii. Speech of Arcadius:—

"Nay, some will swear they love their mistress,
Would hazard lives and fortunes," &c.
Read thus:—

"Nay, some will swear they love their mistress so,
They would hazard lives and fortunes to preserve
One of her hairs brighter than Berenice's,
Or young Apollo's; and yet, after this," &c.
"Thĕy woŭld hāzard"—furnishes an anapæst for an iambus. "And yet," which must be read, anyĕt, is an instance of the enclitic force in an accented monosyllable. "And yēt," is a complete iambus; but anyet is, like spirit, a dibrach u u, trocheized, however, by the arsis or first accent damping, though not extinguishing, the second.

"Wit At Several Weapons."

Act i. Oldcraft's speech:—

"I'm arm'd at all points," &c.
It would be very easy to restore all this passage to metre, by supplying a sentence of four syllables, which the reasoning almost demands, and by correcting the grammar. Read thus:—

"Arm'd at all points 'gainst treachery, I hold
My humour firm. If, living, I can see thee
Thrive by thy wits, I shall have the more courage,
Dying, to trust thee with my lands. If not,
The best wit, I can hear of, carries them.
For since so many in my time and knowledge,
Rich children of the city, have concluded
For lack of wit in beggary, I'd rather
Make a wise stranger my executor,
Than a fool son my heir, and have my lands call'd
After my wit than name: and that's my nature!"
Ib. Oldcraft's speech:—

"To prevent which I have sought out a match for her."
Read—

"Which to prevent I've sought a match out for her."
Ib. Sir Gregory's speech:—

... "Do you think
I'll have any of the wits hang upon me after I am married once?"
Read it thus:—

... "Do you think
That I'll have any of the wits to hang
Upon me after I am married once?"
and afterwards—

... "Is it a fashion in London
To marry a woman, and to never see her?"
The superfluous "to" gives it the Sir Andrew Ague-cheek character.

"The Fair Maid Of The Inn."

Act ii. Speech of Albertus:—

... "But, Sir,
By my life, I vow to take assurance from you,
That right hand never more shall strike my son,
Chop his hand off!"
In this (as, indeed, in all other respects, but most in this) it is that Shakespeare is so incomparably superior to Fletcher and his friend,—in judgment! What can be conceived more unnatural and motiveless than this brutal resolve? How is it possible to feel the least interest in Albertus afterwards? or in Cesario after his conduct?

"The Two Noble Kinsmen."

On comparing the prison scene of Palamon and Arcite, act ii. sc. 2, with the dialogue between the same speakers, act i. sc. 2, I can scarcely retain a doubt as to the first act's having been written by Shakespeare. Assuredly it was not written by B. and F. I hold Jonson more probable than either of these two.

The main presumption, however, for Shakespeare's share in this play rests on a point, to which the sturdy critics of this edition (and indeed all before them) were blind,—that is, the construction of the blank verse, which proves beyond all doubt an intentional imitation, if not the proper hand, of Shakespeare. Now, whatever improbability there is in the former (which supposes Fletcher conscious of the inferiority, the too poematic minus-dramatic nature of his versification, and of which, there is neither proof nor likelihood) adds so much to the probability of the latter. On the other hand, the harshness of many of these very passages, a harshness unrelieved by any lyrical inter-breathings, and still more the want of profundity in the thoughts, keep me from an absolute decision.

Act i. sc. 3. Emilia's speech:—

... "Since his depart, his sports,
Tho' craving seriousness and skill," &c.
I conjecture "imports,"—that is, duties or offices of importance. The flow of the versification in this speech seems to demand the trochaic ending - u; while the text blends jingle and hisses to the annoyance of less sensitive ears than Fletcher's—not to say, Shakespeare's.

"The Woman Hater."

Act i. sc. 2.—

This scene from the beginning is prose printed as blank verse, down to the line—

"E'en all the valiant stomachs in the court"—
where the verse recommences. This transition from the prose to the verse enhances, and indeed forms the comic effect. Lazarillo concludes his soliloquy with a hymn to the goddess of plenty.

THE END.

Note from the Editor

Odin's Library Classics strives to bring you unedited and unabridged works of classical literature. As such, this is the complete and unabridged version of the original English text unless noted. In some instances, obvious typographical errors have been corrected. This is done to preserve the original text as much as possible. The English language has evolved since the writing and some of the words appear in their original form, or at least the most commonly used form at the time. This is done to protect the original intent of the author. If at any time you are unsure of the meaning of a word, please do your research on the etymology of that word. It is important to preserve the history of the English language.

Taylor Anderson

Printed in Great Britain
by Amazon